3 Speak NOW

COMMUNICATE with CONFIDENCE

Jack C. Richards
David Bohlke

OXFORD
UNIVERSITY PRESS

Welcome to Speak NOW

Communicate *with* Confidence

Communicating with confidence means expressing yourself accurately, fluently, and appropriately. **English in Action** lessons throughout the Student Book present video clips which show students how to use target language in real-life settings. The video is available through Oxford Learn Online Practice, DVD, and on the iTools Classroom Presentation Software CD-ROM.

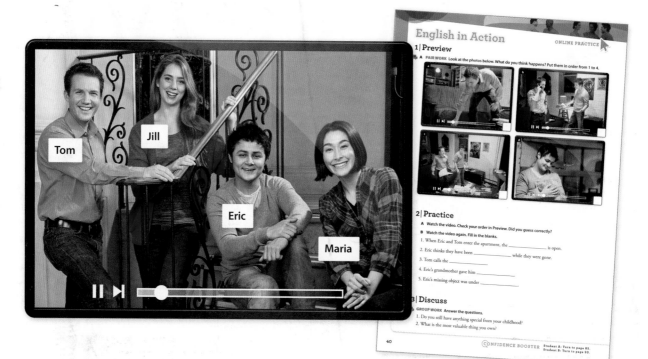

Online Practice powered by oxfordlearn

Speak Now Online Practice features over 100 engaging self-study activities to help you improve your speaking, pronunciation, and listening skills.

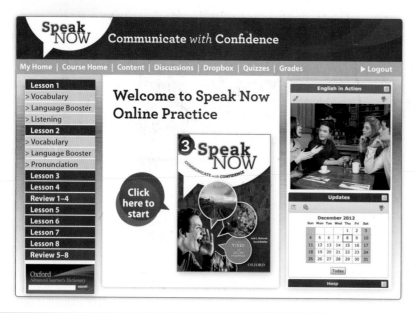

Use the **access card** on the inside back cover to log in at www.oxfordlearn.com/login.

Maximize Speaking

Every activity in every lesson includes a speaking task to ensure students maximize their opportunity to develop confident conversation skills. In each two-page lesson, students learn key **Vocabulary**, practice these new words and develop structured speaking skills through the **Conversation** activity, study new functional language in the **Language Booster** section, and then develop either **Pronunciation** or **Listening** skills in preparation for a communicative **Speak with Confidence** activity.

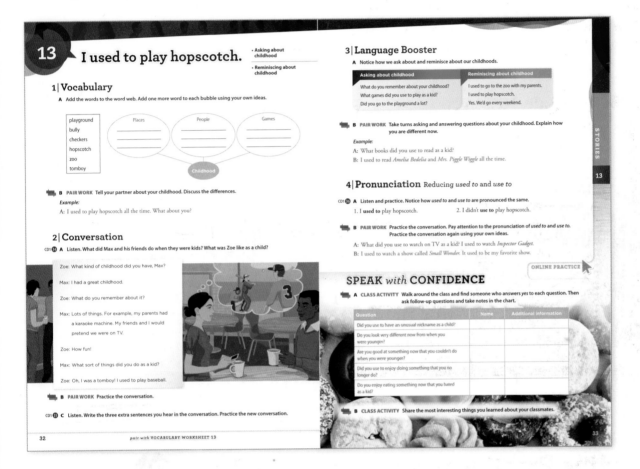

Self-Assessment

Through the **Speak Now** lessons, learners evaluate their progress through role-play situations inspired by the Can-Do statements of the Common European Framework (CEFR).

Scope and Sequence

масштаб Сиквенс - последовательность

Scope and Sequence

CONVERSATION	REVIEW	
	VIDEO	**SELF-ASSESSMENT**

I'm an only child.

• **Asking about family relationships**
....
• **Describing family relationships**

[m ən]

1 Vocabulary

A Read about Alexa's family. Circle the words in the box that apply to her.

Alexa has an older brother and a younger sister. She is not married, but Tom recently proposed to her. They plan to get married next year.

single	only child
engaged	middle child
divorced	firstborn
fiancé/fiancée (fem.)	spouse

B PAIR WORK Tell your partner about your family relationships.

Example:

A: I'm an only child.

B: Not me. I'm a middle child. I have an older brother and a younger sister.

2 | Conversation

CD1 **02** **A Listen. What is Isabel doing today? How many siblings does Isabel have?**

John: Are you waiting for someone?

Isabel: Yeah, my brother. He's going to give me a ride home. We're having a party for my grandmother. It's her 80th birthday.

John: That's nice. Do you have a large family?

Isabel: I guess. Besides my mom and dad, I have three older brothers and two sisters.

John: Wow! You have a big family.

Isabel: Do you have any siblings?

John: No, I'm an only child. It gets lonely sometimes.

Isabel: Really? Sometimes, I want to be alone!

B PAIR WORK Practice the conversation.

CD1 **03** **C Listen. Write the three extra sentences you hear in the conversation. Practice the new conversation.**

3 | Language Booster

A Notice the different ways we ask about and describe family relationships.

Asking about family relationships	Describing family relationships
Do you have · a large family? / any siblings? Are you the firstborn? Who are your family members?	Yes. I have three brothers and a sister. Yes. I have an older brother. No, I'm not. I'm the middle child. I have my grandparents, parents, and two siblings.

B **PAIR WORK** Take turns asking about and describing these people's families.

Rachel	Sam	Tristan
☐ is engaged.	☐ is married with a daughter.	☐ is a middle child.
☐ has an older sister.	☐ has a large extended family.	☐ has a fiancée.

Example:

A: Is Rachel single?

B: No, she is engaged. She has a fiancé.

4 | Pronunciation Stressing important words

CD1 **04** **A** Listen and practice. Notice how we stress the words that carry the most meaning in a sentence.

1. I have an **older brother**.

2. **Sandra** has **never** been **married**.

CD1 **05** **B** Listen. Underline the stressed words. Then practice the sentences.

1. Are you an only child?

2. Roger is the baby of the family.

ONLINE PRACTICE

SPEAK *with* CONFIDENCE

A **PAIR WORK** Find out about each other's families. Ask the questions below or think of your own questions.

Do you have any brothers and sisters? How old are they?

Would you like more siblings? If so, how many?

Who are your parents' siblings? What are they like?

What kind of family would you like to have someday?

B **PAIR WORK** Discuss the similarities and differences in your families.

2 She's a born leader.

1 | Vocabulary

A Complete the sentences. Match the types of people with the correct definitions.

a. role model	c. follower	e. loner	g. pessimist
b. problem solver	d. born leader	f. optimist	h. know-it-all

1. An __ __ feels positively about the future.

2. A _____ feels negatively about the future.

3. A _____ tries to find solutions.

4. A _____ acts as an example to others.

5. A _____ thinks he or she has all the answers.

6. A _____ prefers to be alone.

7. A _____ follows the crowd.

8. A _____ guides or directs others naturally.

B PAIR WORK Tell your partner about people you know who fit the descriptions above.

Example:

A: My best friend is an optimist. She always thinks positively.

B: My dad is my role model.

2 | Conversation

CD1 06 **A** Listen. Who do Andy and Kit think would be the best choice for student union president? What is Richard like?

Andy: Who would be a good person for student union president? _____

Kit: We need someone who has lots of good ideas. How about Amy? She's a born leader. People listen to her.

Andy: And she's an optimist. I like that. _____

Kit: There's also that new student—Richard. What do you think of him? _____

Andy: Well, he's a lot of fun, but he's kind of a know-it-all. _____

Kit: I guess you're right. Let's talk to Amy and see if she's interested.

STUDENT UNION
PRESIDENT ELECTION

B PAIR WORK Practice the conversation. Then find the best places to add the sentences below to the conversation and practice it again.

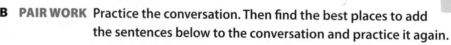

1. I don't think he'd be a good choice. 3. We need someone who is positive.

2. Do you have any ideas? 4. Would he make a good leader?

pair with VOCABULARY WORKSHEET 2

3 | Language Booster

A Notice how we talk about someone's personality type.

Asking about someone's personality type	Describing someone's personality type
What is Amy like?	Amy is a born leader. She's someone who leads naturally. She is someone who people like to be around.
How would you describe Richard?	Richard is an optimist. He's always positive. Richard is a guy that others see as a know-it-all.

B **PAIR WORK** Take turns describing the personality types of two people you know. Use the words and definitions from the Vocabulary section or your own ideas.

4 | Listening

CD1 **07** **A** Listen. Four people are describing themselves. Write the type of person they are in the first column.

	Type	Quality
Maya		
Roberto		
Bernadette		
Young-ho		

CD1 **07** **B** Listen again. What did they say that helped you with your answer? Complete the second column.

ONLINE PRACTICE

SPEAK with CONFIDENCE

A **PAIR WORK** Interview your partner to find out if he or she is a leader or a follower. Check (✓) your partner's answers.

Are you a leader or a follower?	Yes	No
1. Are you usually the first of your friends to try new things?		
2. Do you ignore what's trendy and buy the things you like?		
3. Are you confident in your skills and talents?		
4. Do you feel comfortable making difficult decisions?		
5. Do you get excited by new challenges?		
6. Are you someone that others see as a role model?		

5–6 points: You're definitely a leader.

2–4 points: You're sometimes a leader and sometimes a follower.

0–1 points: You prefer to follow the crowd.

B **PAIR WORK** For every yes answer, add one point. Then check and discuss your results.

3 We're both reliable.

1 | Vocabulary

A Look at the characteristics used to describe people. Mark P (positive) or N (negative).

_____ considerate _____ flexible _____ reliable _____ mature

_____ forgiving _____ moody _____ responsible _____ immature

B **PAIR WORK** Describe your family members using the words above.

Example:

A: My younger sister is flexible. She needs to be more reliable and considerate.

B: That sounds like my brother! He also needs to be more mature.

2 | Conversation

CD1 **08** **A** Listen. Keisha and Kelly are sisters. How are they similar? How are they different?

 Sara: It must be fun having a sister about the same age as you.

 Keisha: Well, sometimes it is.

 Sara: How similar are you and Kelly?

 Keisha: Well, we're both pretty reliable. But I think I'm more reliable than Kelly.

 Sara: Well, you are two years older. How are you different?

 Keisha: She's more flexible than me.

 Sara: What do you mean?

Keisha: She's the type of person who just goes with things. And Kelly is also really forgiving. She lives by the motto, "*Forgive and forget.*"

B **PAIR WORK** Practice the conversation.

CD1 **09** **C** Listen. Write the three extra sentences you hear in the conversation. Practice the new conversation.

pair with VOCABULARY WORKSHEET 3

3 | Language Booster

A Notice the different ways we describe similarities and differences between people.

Describing similarities between people	Describing differences between people
We're both pretty reliable.	I think I'm more reliable than she is.
Both of us are pretty flexible.	She's flexible about things, but I'm not.
	She's more forgiving than me. I'm not as forgiving as she is.

B **PAIR WORK** Check (✓) the true statements about yourself. Then discuss how you and your partner are similar and different.

_____ I'm am a considerate person.   _____ I often get moody when I'm stressed.

_____ I'm not a judgmental person.   _____ I'm very mature for my age.

4 | Pronunciation Stress shifts

CD1 **10** **A** Listen and practice. Notice how the stress shifts when these adjectives become nouns.

1. **flex**ible/flexi**bil**ity   2. re**spon**sible/responsi**bil**ity

CD1 **11** **B** Listen. Mark the stress. Then practice saying the words.

1. mature / maturity   3. sincere / sincerity   5. forgiving / forgiveness

2. generous / generosity   4. reliable / reliability   6. moody / moodiness

ONLINE PRACTICE

SPEAK with CONFIDENCE

A **GROUP WORK** Take turns describing similarities and differences between you and your family members. Answer any questions.

I'm most like my dad. We are both very sociable.

Who are you different from?

I'm really different from my brother.

B **GROUP WORK** Who do you think you are most similar to in your group? Why?

As I was saying...

[ɛ z ɑ ˑ wɛi seiiŋ]

1 | Vocabulary

A Look at the values below. Circle the three most important values to you.

respect   compassion   determination   honesty   kindness

courage   sacrifice   friendship   loyalty   sportsmanship

B **PAIR WORK** Tell your partner who you learn important values from.

Example:

A: I definitely learn about compassion from my parents.

B: I agree. I also learn about compassion from my grandparents.

2 | Conversation

CD1 **12** **A** Listen. Why didn't Megan keep the change the salesclerk gave her? What did the salesclerk do for Megan?

Megan: Hey, Derek. It's me. You'll never guess what happened. _____

Derek: What?

Megan: Well, I was in a department store today, and I found a new dress. When I paid for it, the salesclerk gave me too much change. She gave me *a lot* more—

Derek: Sorry, but can I interrupt for a second? Did you keep the change?

Megan: No, of course not. That wouldn't be honest. I gave it back. _____

Derek: I bet she was happy.

Megan: She was. I didn't want her to lose her job. She was so grateful that she offered me a special discount. _____

Derek: She gave you a discount? _____

Megan: I tried to refuse, but she insisted. I've never experienced such kindness from a stranger before.

B **PAIR WORK** Practice the conversation. Then find the best places to add the sentences below to the conversation and practice it again.

1. Isn't that nice?   3. Did you accept the discount?

2. It's pretty amazing.   4. I know you'd do the same thing.

pair with VOCABULARY WORKSHEET 4

3 | Language Booster

A Notice the different ways we interrupt politely and return to a topic.

Interrupting politely	Returning to a topic
Sorry, but can I interrupt for a second?	Anyway…
I'm sorry, but can I say something?	Anyway, as I was saying…
Excuse me, may I interrupt?	So where was I? Oh…
Excuse me, do you mind if I ask a question?	To get back to what I was saying…

B **PAIR WORK** Take turns discussing one of these topics. Interrupt one another politely. Return to the topic each time.

| this weekend | your favorite movie | an important value |

Example:

A: This past weekend, I went to the mall with my friends. We—

B: Excuse me, but may I interrupt? Who exactly did you go with?

A: I went with Emiko and Peter. Anyway, we had lunch there and…

4 | Listening

CD1 **13** **A** Listen. Rachel is talking about four values that are important to her. Write the values she discusses.

1. _____ 2. _____ 3. _____ 4. _____

CD1 **13** **B** Listen again. How many times do her friends interrupt her? _____

ONLINE PRACTICE

SPEAK *with* CONFIDENCE

A Choose one of the values in the Vocabulary section. Think about the answers to the questions below.

How did you learn it?

Who did you learn this value from?

Is this value especially important to you today?

What are some other ways to teach this value?

B **GROUP WORK** Discuss the values. Don't say the value—let the others guess. Interrupt one another to ask questions.

Example:

A: I learned a value when I found a bird with a broken wing and—

B: Do you mind if I ask a question? How old were you?

A: I was six. Anyway, I wanted to keep the bird, but my mom…

English in Action

ONLINE PRACTICE

1 | Preview

PAIR WORK Look at this photo of Jill. She is going on a trip. Does she pack light? How do you pack when you travel? What do you pack?

2 | Practice

A Watch the video. Mark the statements T (true) or F (false).

_____ 1. Maria, Eric, Tom, and Jill are in New York. _____

_____ 2. Eric's family lives in New York. _____

_____ 3. Tom will stay with Eric's family. _____

_____ 4. Jill and Maria will stay in a hotel. _____

_____ 5. Eric is the oldest child in his family. _____

_____ 6. Eric is Tom's role model. _____

_____ 7. Jill is going away for two weeks. _____

B Watch the video again. Rewrite the false statements so they are true.

3 | Discuss

GROUP WORK Answer the questions.

1. How would you describe Jill?
2. Do you live near your family?
3. Have you traveled recently? Where did you go? Who did you go with?

CONFIDENCE BOOSTER

Student A: Turn to page 82.
Student B: Turn to page 90.

PEOPLE

1

2

3

4

VIDEO

Speak NOW

1 I'm an only child.

Student A and **Student B**: Take turns asking about and describing your families. Discuss your family relationships.

I can ask about family relationships.
☐ Very well ☐ I need more practice.

I can describe family relationships.
☐ Very well ☐ I need more practice.
See Language Booster page 3.

2 She's a born leader.

A Student A: Think of someone in your class who would make a good class representative. Ask Student B about the person.

   Student B: Answer Student A's questions. Say why you think this person would make a good class representative.

B Now change roles.

I can ask about someone's personality type.
☐ Very well ☐ I need more practice.

I can describe someone's personality type.
☐ Very well ☐ I need more practice.
See Language Booster page 5.

3 We're both reliable.

A Student A: Choose someone in your family. Tell Student B about your similarities and differences.

   Student B: Listen to Student A and ask follow-up questions.

B Now change roles.

I can describe similarities between people.
☐ Very well ☐ I need more practice.

I can describe differences between people.
☐ Very well ☐ I need more practice.
See Language Booster page 7.

4 As I was saying...

A Student A: Talk about one of these topics for two minutes. Answer Student B's questions, and then return to the topic.

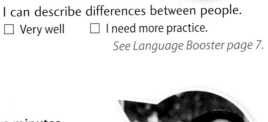

| a person you admire | something you want to be better at |

   Student B: Listen to Student A. Interrupt two times to ask questions.

B Now change roles.

I can interrupt someone politely.
☐ Very well ☐ I need more practice.

I can return to a topic.
☐ Very well ☐ I need more practice.
See Language Booster page 9.

ONLINE PRACTICE

5 I'd like to check in.

• Checking into a hotel

1 | Vocabulary

A Write these travel words in the correct categories. Try to add one more word to each list.

dorm	business center
single	motel
youth hostel	pool
hotel	campground
triple	double

Places to stay	Facilities	Types of rooms

B PAIR WORK Tell your partner which places you have visited and where you stayed.

Example:

A: I went camping last summer and I stayed in a campground.

B: I stayed at a four star hotel in Paris. The hotel restaurant was really good.

2 | Conversation

CD1 **14** **A** Listen. What does Mira provide the hotel clerk? How long is she staying?

Mira: Hello. I'd like to check in, please. My name's Mira Abboud.

Hotel clerk: Yes, I have your reservation here, Ms. Abboud.
May I have your passport?

Mira: Here you are. By the way, is there wireless Internet in the room?

Hotel clerk: Yes, but for a fee. It's free in the lobby. Can I have
your credit card, please?

Mira: Sure.

Hotel clerk: Thank you. Let me confirm this for you. You have
a single room for four nights, checking out on the 16th.
Is there anything more I can do for you?

Mira: I don't think so. Thank you.

Hotel clerk: You're welcome. Enjoy your stay.

B PAIR WORK Practice the conversation.

CD1 **15** **C** Listen. Write the three extra sentences you hear in the conversation. Practice the new conversation.

pair with VOCABULARY WORKSHEET 5

3 | Language Booster

A Notice how we check into a hotel.

Checking into a hotel	Responding
Do you have a reservation?	Yes, I do.
Are you here for four nights?	That's right.
Is one queen-size bed OK?	Yes, that'll be fine.
Can I have your credit card, please?	Yes, here you are.
May I see your passport, please?	Of course. Here you go.
Could you fill in this form?	Yes, of course.

B PAIR WORK Take turns checking into a hotel. Use the ideas below.

pool	ID card	restaurant	business center	double room

4 | Pronunciation Linking sounds

CD1 16 **A** Listen and practice. Notice how consonant sounds at the end of words are linked to the vowel sounds that follow them.

1. Do you ha**ve a** reservation?

2. Could you fi**ll in** this card?

B PAIR WORK Practice these sentences and questions. Pay attention to linked sounds.

1. Ca**n I** have you**r I**D card?

2. Wireles**s is** free he**re in** the lobby.

3. Plea**se e**njoy your stay wi**th u**s.

4. Is the**re a**nything mo**re I** can do?

ONLINE PRACTICE

SPEAK with CONFIDENCE

A PAIR WORK Fill in the information below. Then take turns practicing the conversation between a hotel clerk and a guest.

Hotel clerk: Hello. Can I help you?

Guest: _____

Hotel clerk: Certainly. Do you have a reservation?

Guest: _____

Hotel clerk: Ah yes. Here's your name. Can I see your I.D.?

Guest: _____

Hotel clerk: Thank you. And could you fill in this registration card?

Guest: _____

Hotel clerk: Is there anything more I can do for you?

Guest: _____

6 Here are some rules.

• Saying what is allowed
• Saying what is not allowed

1 | Vocabulary

A Look at these rules. Where can you find them? Mark H (hotel), Y (youth hostel), or B (both).

_____ 1. Leave the **key** at the front desk.

_____ 2. No **noise** after midnight.

_____ 3. Shower before entering the **pool.**

_____ 4. Kitchen for **guests** only.

_____ 5. Shared **bathrooms** on each floor.

_____ 6. **Health club** hours: 10 a.m.–8 p.m.

_____ 7. Safe in room for **valuables.**

_____ 8. 11 p.m. **curfew.**

_____ 9. 10% discount for **members.**

_____ 10. Call 0 for **room service.**

B PAIR WORK Tell your partner where you might find the rules above.

Example:

A: There is probably an 11 p.m. curfew in youth hostels.

2 | Conversation

CD1 **17** **A** Listen. What's an important rule at the hostel? What can guests do?

Manager: Here's your membership card. Let me just mention an important rule.

Jun: Oh, sure. _____

Manager: You can't make noise after midnight. _____

Jun: OK. By the way, is there a kitchen?

Manager: Yes. There's one on each floor. You're allowed to use the kitchen any time. _____

Jun: So, I can cook?

Manager: Yes. And you can help yourself to tea in the lobby all day. Here is your key. _____

B PAIR WORK Practice the conversation. Then find the best places to add the sentences below to the conversation and practice it again.

1. I didn't know there were any rules.

2. Enjoy your stay.

3. Be sure to keep it clean.

4. That means no loud music.

3 | Language Booster

A Notice the different ways we describe things that are allowed and not allowed.

Saying what is allowed	Saying what is not allowed
You can help yourself to tea and coffee. You're allowed to use the kitchen. It's OK to play music quietly.	You can't make noise after midnight. You're not allowed to have parties. No one is permitted to have guests.

B **PAIR WORK** Look at the list of rules. Take turns describing what is and isn't allowed.

Example:

A: You can have guests until 8 p.m.

B: Right. You're not allowed to have guests after 8 p.m.

> **Youth hostel rules**
> * Guests until 8 p.m. only
> * No loud music
> * Kitchen open 24 hours
> * Lights out by 10 p.m.

4 | Listening

CD1 **18** **A** Listen. Sandra has just moved into a new apartment. Number the topics she discusses with the building manager from 1 to 4 in the order you hear them. There is one extra.

_____ a. parking   _____ b. guests   _____ c. pets   _____ d. parties   _____ e. curfew

CD1 **18** **B** Listen again. Write one rule for each topic.

1. parking: _____   3. pets: _____

2. guests: _____   4. parties: _____

C **PAIR WORK** Tell your partner the rules you need to follow in your neighborhood.

ONLINE PRACTICE

SPEAK *with* CONFIDENCE

A **PAIR WORK** What are some things you are allowed to do in your English class? What aren't you allowed to do? What do you think of these rules?

> We're allowed to use a dictionary app in class.

> But we can't answer our phones.

B **CLASS ACTIVITY** Agree on rules for your English class. Use these and your own ideas.

mobile phones	homework	classroom behavior
on time	seating	dress code

> ✳ **CLASS RULES** ✳
> ✓ Arrive on time, or pay a fine!
> ✓ English only (try your best!)
> ✓ **No mobile phones**
> ✓ Homework once a week only
> ✓ Sit with a different partner every day
> ✓ Raise your hand if you want to speak

There are some problems.

1 | Vocabulary

A Match the items in a hotel room to the complaints.

a. TV	b. bed	c. sink	d. shower	e. closet	f. desk	g. toilet	h. lamp

_____ 1. There is no hot water.

_____ 2. There aren't any hangers.

_____ 3. It won't flush.

_____ 4. The faucet is leaking.

_____ 5. It's too soft.

_____ 6. The lightbulb is burned out.

_____ 7. The drawer won't open.

_____ 8. The remote doesn't work.

B **PAIR WORK** Tell your partner some other complaints a guest might have for the items above.

Example:

A: The volume isn't working. There's no sound.

2 | Conversation

CD1 ⑲ **A** Listen. What three things are wrong in the hotel room? How does the hotel clerk solve the last problem?

Hotel clerk: Front desk. How can I help you?

Guest: Hi, I just checked in. There are some problems with my room.

Hotel clerk: Oh, sorry to hear that. What are the problems?

Guest: Well, first the bedside lamp isn't working at all.

Hotel clerk: It may need a new lightbulb.

Guest: That's what I thought. And the faucet in the bathroom is leaking.

Hotel clerk: OK. I'll get someone to come and look at it right away.

Guest: Thank you. And one more thing. There are no towels in the bathroom.

Hotel clerk: I'll ask housekeeping to send you some now.

Guest: Great. I really appreciate it.

Hotel clerk: Thank you for your patience.

B **PAIR WORK** Practice the conversation.

CD1 ⑳ **C** Listen. Write the three extra sentences you hear in the conversation. Practice the new conversation.

3 | Language Booster

A Notice how we talk about and address problems.

Stating problems	Addressing problems
The bedside lamp isn't working.	It may need a new lightbulb.
The shower and sink are very dirty.	Let me get someone to come and clean it.
The faucet in the bathroom is leaking.	I'll get someone to look at it.
I need another towel in the bathroom.	I'll ask housekeeping to send you some right away.

B **PAIR WORK** Take turns stating and addressing hotel room problems. Use the ideas from the Vocabulary section or your own ideas.

Example:

A: The remote control isn't working.

B: It may need batteries. I'll get someone to look at it.

4 | Pronunciation Reduction of *and*

CD1 **21** **A** Listen and practice. Notice how *and* is often reduced to /ən/.

1. The shower and sink are very dirty. 2. I'll get someone to come and look at it.

B **PAIR WORK** Complete and practice these sentences. Pay attention to the reduction of *and*.

1. The sink and _____ are very dirty.

2. The TV and _____ aren't working in my room.

3. The sandwich and _____ are delicious!

ONLINE PRACTICE

SPEAK *with* CONFIDENCE

A Your class is on a school trip. Look at the picture. You are in a hotel room with a lot of problems. List five complaints about the room.

1. _____.

2. _____.

3. _____.

4. _____.

5. _____.

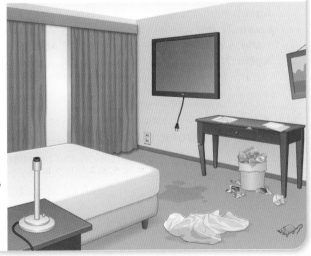

B **PAIR WORK** Take turns stating the problems and addressing them. Are you happy with the solutions?

8 That would be great.

• Offering help

• Accepting and declining help

1 | Vocabulary

A Complete the sentences. Match the people to the things they might do.

a. restaurant server	c. flight attendant	e. salesclerk	g. train reservations agent
b. parking attendant	d. bus driver	f. hotel clerk	h. travel agent

1. A __b__ gets your car.

2. A _____ changes your room.

3. A _____ wraps your purchase.

4. A _____ reserves a spot on a city tour.

5. A _____ books a sleeper car.

6. A _____ indicates your stop.

7. A _____ brings a dessert menu.

8. A _____ takes your tray.

B PAIR WORK Tell your partner other things the people above might do.

2 | Conversation

CD1 22 **A** Listen. Where does Laura want to go? Who is going to mail the postcards?

Laura: Hi. Do you have a city map? _____
Agent: Here you go.
Laura: Thank you. Is it far to the museum?
Agent: No. I can draw the route for you if you'd like.

Laura: That would be great. And do you have information on day trips to the mountains?
Agent: Yes. A tour bus company does that. _____
Laura: That sounds great. _____

Agent: Is there anything else I can help you with?
Laura: Yes. Where can I mail these postcards?
Agent: Do you want me to mail them for you?
Laura: Sure. I'd appreciate that. _____

B PAIR WORK Practice the conversation. Then find the best places to add the sentences below to the conversation and practice it again.

1. The tour is $42.   3. But I want to try the walking tour.

2. Thank you for all your help.   4. It's my first day here.

3 | Language Booster

A Notice the different ways we offer, accept, and decline help.

Offering help		Accepting help
I can / I'd be happy to	call a taxi for you.	That would be great. / Sure. I'd appreciate that.
		Declining help
Do you want me to / Would you like me to	reserve a spot for you?	That won't be necessary. / No, that's OK.

B **PAIR WORK** Take turns offering help, and either accepting or declining help. Use the ideas from the Vocabulary section.

4 | Listening

CD1 **23** **A** Listen to people offering to help. Who is offering to do each thing? Number the people from 1–5 in the order you hear them offering help. There is one extra person.

_____ a. a restaurant server   _____ c. a parking attendant   _____ e. a flight attendant

_____ b. a bus driver   _____ d. a salesclerk   _____ f. hotel clerk

CD1 **23** **B** Listen again. What do the people offer to do? Complete the sentences.

1. He offers to _____.

2. She offers to _____.

3. He offers to _____.

4. She offers to _____.

5. He offers to _____.

ONLINE PRACTICE

SPEAK with CONFIDENCE

CLASS ACTIVITY Walk around and read aloud each statement. Write two different offers for each statement you hear from others. Accept or decline the offers.

Statement	Offer 1	Offer 2
I don't know when the movie starts.		
I need directions to the party.		
I didn't do my homework.		
My cell phone battery is dead.		
I am really hungry.		

I need directions to the party.

Oh, I can draw you a map.

English in Action

1 | Preview

PAIR WORK Look at the photo below. Where are Maria and Jill? What are they doing? Write down two guesses.

1. _____   2. _____

2 | Practice

A Watch the video. Answer the questions.

1. What is Jill's correct last name? Spell it correctly. _____

2. What two things does Jill hand the clerk? _____

3. What two types of drinks are available in the room? _____

4. What two things are not allowed? _____

B Watch the video again. Write the one problem Jill mentions to the hotel clerk over the phone.

_____

3 | Discuss

GROUP WORK Answer the questions.

1. Do people ever have problems spelling or saying your name? Do you usually correct them?

2. Do you think it is OK for a hotel to ask that there be no parties?

3. Have you ever lost power? What did you do?

VACATION

5

6

7

8

VIDEO

CONFIDENCE BOOSTER   Student A: Turn to page 83.
Student B: Turn to page 91.

5 I'd like to check in.

A Student A: You are checking into a hotel. Student B is the hotel clerk. Ask and answer questions.

Student B: You are a hotel clerk. Student A is a guest. Help him or her check in.

B Now change roles.

I can check into a hotel.
☐ Very well   ☐ I need more practice.

See Language Booster page 13.

6 Here are some rules.

A Student A: You work at a gym. Student B is a guest. Tell him or her about the rules.

Student B: You are a guest at a gym. Student A works there. Listen to the rules. Ask follow-up questions.

B Now change roles.

CLASS RULES ➤
✓ Arrive on time, or pay a fine!
✓ English only (try your best!)
✓ No mobile phones
✓ Homework once a week only
✓ Sit with a different partner every day
✓ Raise your hand if you want to speak

I can describe things that are allowed.
☐ Very well   ☐ I need more practice.

I can describe things that are not allowed.
☐ Very well   ☐ I need more practice.

See Language Booster page 15.

7 There are some problems.

A Student A: You are at a restaurant, but there are problems. Student B is a manager. State the problems.

Student B: You are a manager in a restaurant. Student A is eating there. Address the problems he or she states.

B Now change roles.

I can state problems.
☐ Very well   ☐ I need more practice.

I can address problems.
☐ Very well   ☐ I need more practice.

See Language Booster page 17.

8 That would be great.

A Student A: Offer to do three things for Student B.

Student B: Refuse two of the offers Student A makes. Accept one offer.

B Now change roles.

I can offer help.
☐ Very well   ☐ I need more practice.

I can accept or decline help.
☐ Very well   ☐ I need more practice.

See Language Booster page 19.

ONLINE PRACTICE

Do you know...?

1 | Vocabulary

A Match the places with questions you might have while you are there.

a. health food store ✓	c. hair salon	e. food court	g. electronics store
b. office supply store ✓	d. travel agency	f. boutique	h. dry cleaners

_____ 1. Which TVs are on sale?

_____ 2. Do you have this in a different color?

_____ 3. Can you remove this stain?

_____ 4. Where is your printing paper?

_____ 5. Are these vegetables organic?

_____ 6. How long will a cut and blow dry take?

_____ 7. Do I need to reconfirm my flight?

_____ 8. Does the lunch special include a drink?

B **PAIR WORK** Tell your partner what each place sells or offers.

2 | Conversation

CD1 **24** **A** Listen. What doesn't Anne like about her town? What does Mark need to do this weekend?

Mark: So, what's it like living here? It looks like a convenient place to live.

Anne: Oh, it is. The only thing is there's a lot of construction. But I really like it, and everything I need is close by.

Mark: Sounds great! Actually, I need to do a few things this weekend. Do you know where I can get a haircut?

Anne: I'd go to Paul's Hair Salon just down the street. It's really popular.

Mark: And do you know if it's expensive?

Anne: I don't think so. A haircut is $20 or so.

Mark: That's not too bad. Where is it?

Anne: It's next to Super Foods. You can take a bus there.

B **PAIR WORK** Practice the conversation.

CD1 **25** **C** Listen. Write the three extra sentences you hear in the conversation. Practice the new conversation.

pair with VOCABULARY WORKSHEET 9

3 | Language Booster

A Notice the different ways we ask and respond to indirect questions.

Asking indirect questions		Responding
Do you know / Can you tell me	how much the bus is?	It's two dollars.
	what bus I need?	You need bus number 14.
	where I can get a haircut?	I'd go to Paul's Hair Salon.
	if it's expensive?	A haircut is $20 or so.
	if the buses run late?	I think they run until 11:00.
	if I can use a credit card?	Sorry. I have no idea.

B **PAIR WORK** Take turns asking and answering questions that start with *Do you know…* and *Can you tell me…*

Example:

A: Can you tell me if there's a food court near here?

B: Yes, there's one in the basement of Lind's Department Store.

4 | Pronunciation Intonation when requesting information

CD1 26 **A** Listen and practice. Notice how intonation rises when requesting information.

1. Do you know how much the bus is?   2. Can you tell me if the buses run late?

B **PAIR WORK** Take turns asking and answering the questions in the Language Booster section. Work with a new partner. Pay attention to the intonation.

ONLINE PRACTICE

SPEAK with CONFIDENCE

A What do you want to know about your neighborhood or city? Complete these questions.

Questions	Student 1	Student 2
1. Do you know _____ ?		
2. Can you tell me _____ ?		
3. Do you know _____ ?		
4. Can you tell me _____ ?		

B **CLASS ACTIVITY** Walk around the class and ask each of your questions to two different people. Take notes on their answers.

C **GROUP WORK** Share your results. Did your classmates have similar or different answers? Were there questions that neither person could answer? Can anyone in your group answer them?

Sorry. My mistake.

1 | Vocabulary

A Look at some ways people point out mistakes. Complete the sentences with the correct words.

overcharged
receipt
misspelled
change
missing
undercharged

1. This is the wrong _____. It belongs to that shopper.

2. The rice is _____. Can someone deliver it right away?

3. You forgot my _____. I should get two dollars back.

4. You _____ me. I should get another $10 back.

5. You _____ my name on the ticket.

6. You _____ me. I gave you $10, not $20. This is yours.

B **PAIR WORK** Tell your partner if you had to point out any mistakes recently.

2 | Conversation

CD1 27 **A** Listen. How much did the customer give the clerk? How much change did he get back?

Clerk: Hello. All set?
Customer: Yes. _____
Clerk: Will that be cash or credit?
Customer: I'll pay with cash.
Clerk: That comes to $35.
Customer: Here you are.

Clerk: Thank you. And here's your change.
Customer: Um, I think you gave me the wrong change.
Clerk: Really? _____
Customer: I gave you $50.

Clerk: Right. _____
Customer: You gave me only two five-dollar bills.
Clerk: Oh, I'm sorry. My mistake. I thought there were three bills there. _____
Customer: No problem.

B **PAIR WORK** Practice the conversation. Then find the best places to add the sentences below to the conversation and practice it again.

1. Are you sure?	3. Just this sweater, please.
2. Here's the correct change.	4. And how much did I give you?

3 | Language Booster

A Notice the different ways we point out mistakes and apologize.

Pointing out mistakes politely	Apologizing for mistakes
I think	Oh, I'm sorry.
I'm afraid you gave me the wrong change.	Sorry. My mistake.
It seems	Really? I'm so sorry.
I'm sorry, but I don't think this is the correct change.	Please accept my apologies.

B PAIR WORK Take turns pointing out mistakes and apologizing. Use the words from the Vocabulary section or your own ideas.

Example:

A: I'm afraid this is the wrong order. I ordered spaghetti.

B: Oh, I'm sorry. Let me take that, and I'll be right back with your meal.

4 | Listening

CD1 **28** **A** Listen. It's Frank's first day on the job as a waiter. Listen and number the pictures from 1 to 4 in the order you hear things happen.

CD1 **28** **B** Listen again. How does Frank solve each problem? Write the solutions.

1. _____

2. _____

3. _____

4. _____

ONLINE PRACTICE

SPEAK with CONFIDENCE

PAIR WORK Take turns pointing out these mistakes and apologizing. Find solutions to the problems.

The price on an item was $15, but you were charged $18.

An item was on sale, but you didn't get the 20% discount.

You bought three items, but you were only charged for two of them.

You ordered a large pizza, but a medium was delivered.

25

Can I please...?

1 | Vocabulary

A Match the jobs to the types of appointments.

a. hairstylist	c. veterinarian	e. career counselor	g. wedding planner
b. computer technician	d. photographer	f. academic adviser	h. doctor

_____ 1. to discuss jobs good for me

_____ 2. to bring in my cat for a shot

_____ 3. to see what courses I need to graduate

_____ 4. to get my hair colored

_____ 5. to talk about my marriage plans

_____ 6. to get my laptop repaired

_____ 7. to have a professional portrait taken

_____ 8. to get a check-up

B PAIR WORK Discuss how you make appointments to see the people above.

Example:

A: I'd make an appointment with a computer technician by phone.

B: I make appointments with my hair stylist in person.

2 | Conversation

CD1 **29** **A Listen. When is Heather's appointment? What time should she arrive?**

Receptionist: Good morning. Dr. Kim's office.

Heather: Hello. I'd like to make an appointment to see Dr. Kim.

Receptionist: What is your name, please?

Heather: Heather Jenson.

Receptionist: I can get you an appointment this Thursday. Can you come in at 11:15?

Heather: Um...I'd prefer something in the afternoon.

Receptionist: Would you be able to come in on Friday at 3:30?

Heather: Let me see...yes, that's fine.

Receptionist. OK. So your appointment is with Dr. Kim at 3:30 on Friday the 20th. Please come about 15 minutes early.

Heather: Great! Thank you.

B PAIR WORK Practice the conversation.

CD1 **30** **C Listen. Write the three extra sentences you hear in the conversation. Practice the new conversation.**

pair with VOCABULARY WORKSHEET 11

3 | Language Booster

A Notice the different ways we make appointments and confirm information.

Making appointments	Responding
I'd like to make an appointment, please.	Certainly.
Can I please make an appointment?	What time are you free?
Is it possible for me to make an appointment to see the doctor?	Let me see what's available.

Confirming information	
Your appointment is with Dr. Kim at 3:30 on Friday the 20th.	
To confirm, your appointment with Dr. Kim is next Friday at 3:30.	

B **PAIR WORK** Take turns making appointments with the people in the Vocabulary section.

4 | Pronunciation Reduction of *let me* and *give me*

CD1 31 **A** **Listen and practice. Notice how *let me* and *give me* are sometimes reduced.**

/lemme/
1. Let me just confirm that.

/gimme/
2. Could you give me your phone number?

B **PAIR WORK** Practice saying the sentences below. Pay attention to the reduction of *let me* and *give me*.

A: Can you give me your phone number?

B: Let me see…it's 992-8713. Could you give me yours?

A: Let me just call you now.

ONLINE PRACTICE

SPEAK *with* CONFIDENCE

A Look at the jobs below. Think of a reason to see them in the next few days.

a hairstylist	a dentist	a doctor	a career counselor

B **GROUP WORK** Take turns asking for appointments with the people in part A. Write down the details.

Name	Reason	Time

C **CLASS ACTIVITY** Share details about your appointments.

12 I'm broke.

• **Making recommendations**

• **Acknowledging recommendations**

1 | Vocabulary

A Look at the problems people can have. Find a suggestion for the problem.

a. I'm broke.	c. I'm stressed.	e. I'm forgetful.	g. I'm sick.
b. I'm sleepy.	d. I'm lonely.	f. I'm depressed.	h. I'm overwhelmed.

_____ 1. Join a social network.

_____ 2. Spend less.

_____ 3. Go to bed earlier.

_____ 4. Take up meditation.

_____ 5. See a doctor.

_____ 6. Do one thing at a time.

_____ 7. Get out more.

_____ 8. Write things down.

B **PAIR WORK** Tell your partner other things you can do for the problems above.

2 | Conversation

CD1 **32** **A** Listen. How are Calvin and his roommate Ben going to save money for their trip?

 Calvin: We still need some more money for our trip to Italy. _____

 Ben: I know. We're broke.

 Calvin: One thing we should do is to stop our gym memberships for a few months. _____

 Ben: That's a good idea, but I go to the gym every day. We could eat at home instead of going out to eat so much. _____

 Calvin: I hadn't thought of that. How about spending less on movies, too? _____

 Ben: I like that idea, but life is going to be pretty boring for the next few months, isn't it?

B **PAIR WORK** Practice the conversation. Then find the best places to add the sentences below to the conversation and practice it again.

1. Movie tickets are so expensive.	3. I bet that would help a lot.
2. Our finances aren't looking so good.	4. The membership is so expensive.

3 | Language Booster

A Notice the different ways we make and acknowledge recommendations.

Making recommendations		Acknowledging recommendations
One thing we should do is Something else we could do is We could	stop our gym membership. eat at home more often.	I hadn't thought of that. That's a good idea. I like that idea. I'm not so sure about that. I don't really like that idea.

B **PAIR WORK** Take turns making and acknowledging recommendations for these problems.

You forgot your homework.	You're angry at your friend.	You want to get a job.

4 | Listening

CD1 **33** **A** Listen. Check (✓) the recommendations that Dylan makes to his friend Lindsay.

☐ 1. stop taking buses   ☐ 6. take out books from the library

☐ 2. walk when possible   ☐ 7. buy only clothes that are on sale

☐ 3. bring lunch to school   ☐ 8. keep a daily budget

☐ 4. drink less coffee and soda   ☐ 9. cut up her credit cards

☐ 5. cancel magazine subscriptions

CD1 **33** **B** Listen again. Underline the recommendations that Lindsay likes.

C **PAIR WORK** Tell your partner if you think the recommendations in part A are good or not.

ONLINE PRACTICE

SPEAK with CONFIDENCE

A **PAIR WORK** Look at these ideas from a student handbook on ways to save money. Take turns making recommendations. Which ones do you feel are good ideas?

Expenses	Ways to save
Books/magazines	Read things online.
Food/beverages	Eat at home.
Entertainment	Watch movies on your computer.
Shopping	Wait for sales.
Transportation	Walk more.

B **GROUP WORK** Take turns making additional recommendations. Vote on the best one.

English in Action

ONLINE PRACTICE

1 | Preview

Maria and Jill want to do something exciting in New York. Check (✓) two places you would like to visit.

2 | Practice

A Watch the video. Write answers to the questions.

1. What does the hotel clerk say they should do in Central Park? _____

2. What does the hotel clerk say about prices in the East Village? _____

3. What time of day does the hotel clerk suggest they go to Times Square? _____

4. What does the hotel clerk think is fun to do in Soho? _____

B PAIR WORK Compare your answers with your partner.

3 | Discuss

GROUP WORK Answer the questions.

1. What do you recommend people do when they visit your city or town?

2. Have you ever traveled with a friend? Where did you go? What did you do?

3. Who cuts your hair? Have you ever tried something very different?

CONFIDENCE BOOSTER

Student A: Turn to page 84.
Student B: Turn to page 92.

ERRANDS

9

10

11

12

VIDEO

9 ▸ Do you know...?

A Student A: Ask Student B three indirect questions about places in his or her hometown.

Student B: Answer Student A's questions.

B Now change roles.

I can ask indirect questions.
☐ Very well   ☐ I need more practice.

See Language Booster page 23.

10 ▸ Sorry. My mistake.

A Student A: You are shopping. Student B is a salesclerk and overcharged you. Point out the mistake politely.

Student B: You are a salesclerk. Apologize for the mistake Student A points out to you. Fix the mistake.

B Now change roles. This time the salesclerk undercharges.

I can point out a mistake politely.
☐ Very well   ☐ I need more practice.

I can apologize for a mistake.
☐ Very well   ☐ I need more practice.

See Language Booster page 25.

11 ▸ Can I please...?

A Student A: You want to get a professional photo taken. Student B is a photographer. Call and make an appointment.

Student B: You are a busy photographer. Student A calls to make an appointment. Make and confirm the appointment.

B Now change roles. Student A is a famous wedding planner.

I can make an appointment.
☐ Very well   ☐ I need more practice.

I can confirm information.
☐ Very well   ☐ I need more practice.

See Language Booster page 27.

12 ▸ I'm broke.

A Student A: You want to save money. Tell Student B. Acknowledge the recommendations you hear.

Student B: Listen to Student A and make recommendations.

B Now change roles. Student B wants to eat healthier.

I can make recommendations.
☐ Very well   ☐ I need more practice.

I can acknowledge recommendations.
☐ Very well   ☐ I need more practice.

See Language Booster page 29.

ONLINE PRACTICE

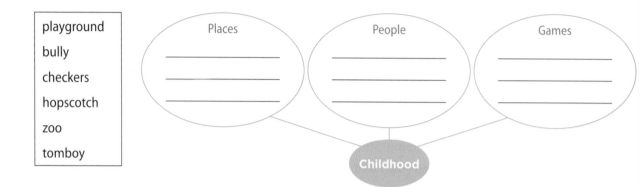

13 | I used to play hopscotch.

- **Asking about childhood**
- **Reminiscing about childhood**

1 | Vocabulary

A Add the words to the word web. Add one more word to each bubble using your own ideas.

playground
bully
checkers
hopscotch
zoo
tomboy

Places
_____
_____
_____

People
_____
_____
_____

Games
_____
_____
_____

Childhood

B **PAIR WORK** Tell your partner about your childhood. Discuss the differences.

Example:

A: I used to play hopscotch all the time. What about you?

2 | Conversation

CD1 **34** **A** Listen. What did Max and his friends do when they were kids? What was Zoe like as a child?

Zoe: What kind of childhood did you have, Max?

Max: I had a great childhood.

Zoe: What do you remember about it?

Max: Lots of things. For example, my parents had a karaoke machine. My friends and I would pretend we were on TV.

Zoe: How fun!

Max: What sort of things did you do as a kid?

Zoe: Oh, I was a tomboy! I used to play baseball.

B **PAIR WORK** Practice the conversation.

CD1 **35** **C** Listen. Write the three extra sentences you hear in the conversation. Practice the new conversation.

pair with VOCABULARY WORKSHEET 13

3 | Language Booster

A Notice how we ask about and reminisce about our childhoods.

Asking about childhood	Reminiscing about childhood
What do you remember about your childhood?	I used to go to the zoo with my parents.
What games did you use to play as a kid?	I used to play hopscotch.
Did you go to the playground a lot?	Yes. We'd go every weekend.

B **PAIR WORK** Take turns asking and answering questions about your childhood. Explain how you are different now.

Example:

A: What books did you use to read as a kid?

B: I used to read *Amelia Bedelia* and *Mrs. Piggle Wiggle* all the time.

4 | **Pronunciation** Reducing *used to* and *use to*

CD1 **36** **A** Listen and practice. Notice how *used to* and *use to* are pronounced the same.

1. I **used to** play hopscotch.

2. I didn't **use to** play hopscotch.

B **PAIR WORK** Practice the conversation. Pay attention to the pronunciation of *used to* and *use to*. Practice the conversation again using your own ideas.

A: What did you use to watch on TV as a kid? I used to watch *Inspector Gadget*.

B: I used to watch a show called *Small Wonder*. It used to be my favorite show.

ONLINE PRACTICE

SPEAK *with* CONFIDENCE

A **CLASS ACTIVITY** Walk around the class and find someone who answers *yes* to each question. Then ask follow-up questions and take notes in the chart.

Question	Name	Additional information
Did you use to have an unusual nickname as a child?		
Do you look very different now from when you were younger?		
Are you good at something now that you couldn't do when you were younger?		
Did you use to enjoy doing something that you no longer do?		
Do you enjoy eating something now that you hated as a kid?		

B **CLASS ACTIVITY** Share the most interesting things you learned about your classmates.

14 She said she was sorry.

1 | Vocabulary

A Match the best reaction to the different situations.

_____ 1. How lucky!   a. Four people in my English class have the same birthday as me.

_____ 2. How strange!   b. I wore two different color socks all day, and didn't realize it.

_____ 3. How awful!   c. My brother proposed to his girlfriend in Paris!

_____ 4. How embarrassing!   d. My neighbor entered a contest and won a free trip to Hawaii.

_____ 5. How scary!   e. My uncle lost his job, and he can't find another one.

_____ 6. How disgusting!   f. My friend was stuck for one hour on a roller coaster.

_____ 7. How romantic!   g. My roommate ate a large pizza last night all by himself.

B **PAIR WORK** Take turns continuing the situations above with your own ideas to make a story.

2 | Conversation

CD1 **37** **A** Listen. What did Alex's friend want? Why was Alex embarrassed?

Alex: Something really embarrassing happened to me on Saturday. I was having dinner with a friend. at Lulu's. _____
Carrie: I know that place. My cousin said they had great food.

Alex: Yeah, they do. Anyway, I saw someone famous at the next table—Rihanna! _____
Carrie: No way! She's one of my favorite singers. She has a fantastic voice. _____

Alex: My friend wanted an autograph. So, I said I would ask her.
Carrie: And did you?
Alex: Yes, but she told me she wasn't Rihanna!
Carrie: How embarrassing! _____

B **PAIR WORK** Practice the conversation. Then find the best places to add the sentences below to the conversation and practice it again.

1. I couldn't believe it.   3. It's that new place on First Avenue.

2. Did you talk to her?   4. But I bet she found it funny.

3 | Language Booster

A Notice how we report what someone said.

Comment	Reporting what someone said
I'm sorry.	She said she was sorry.
They have good food there.	He told me they had good food there.
He arrived at 8:30.	He said he had arrived at 8:30.
I haven't been here for long.	She said she hadn't been there for long.
I will ask her for an autograph.	I said I would ask her for an autograph.

B **PAIR WORK** Take turns completing these sentences with your own ideas and reacting. Use the expressions from the Vocabulary section.

My mother told me that she was planning to _____.

My friend said he found a _____.

4 | Listening

CD1 38 **A** Listen. Inez is telling Chelsea some good news. Mark the statements T (true) or F (false).

_____ 1. Inez told Chelsea she had entered a magazine contest. _____

_____ 2. Inez said the prize was a trip to New Zealand. _____

_____ 3. Inez said she remembered entering the contest. _____

_____ 4. She said the trip would be for two weeks. _____

_____ 5. Inez said she wanted Chelsea to go on the trip with her. _____

CD1 38 **B** Listen again. Rewrite the false statements to make them true.

C **PAIR WORK** Have you ever had something lucky happen to you? Tell your partner about it.

ONLINE PRACTICE

SPEAK with CONFIDENCE

A Choose two of these sentences and complete them.

I am very good at _____.

I talked to _____ on the phone yesterday.

I am going to _____ after class today.

Next year, I will _____.

B **GROUP WORK** Quietly say a sentence to the person on the right. That person quietly says your sentence to the person on his or her right. Continue until the sentence is reported back to you. Was it the same sentence or was it different?

15 I read an unusual story.

• Talking about news

• Adding information

1 | Vocabulary

A Look at the news headlines below. Complete the headlines with the correct words.

saves	closes	scores	donates	crashes
cancels	denies	catches	breaks	causes

1. Actress _____ marriage rumors.

2. Woman _____ leg after ski accident.

3. Storm _____ millions in damages.

4. Truck _____ into store window.

5. Teen _____ $10,000 to charity.

6. Boy _____ family from fire.

7. Network _____ all reality shows.

8. Stock market _____ higher.

9. Young fan _____ second baseball.

10. Soccer star _____ five goals.

B **PAIR WORK** Tell your partner which stories interest you and which don't.

2 | Conversation

CD1 **39** **A** Listen. Who is Cameron Titus? What charity has he donated money to?

Aaron: I saw an interesting news story about a 10-year-old boy who wrote a children's book. His name is Cameron Titus and the book is called *Cameron's A-Z.*

Molly: Really?

Aaron: The towns near him had some bad storms. He wanted to help, so he donated all the money he made to the charity, Habitat for Humanity.

Molly: What a great kid.

Aaron: He's already started to write a second book, too. He's donating all that money as well—to a local hospital.

B **PAIR WORK** Practice the conversation.

CD1 **40** **C** Listen. Write the three extra sentences you hear in the conversation. Practice the new conversation.

3 | Language Booster

A Notice the different ways we talk about news and add information.

Talking about news	Adding information
I saw something interesting on TV last night.	Also, he's donating all the money to charity.
I read an unusual story online earlier today.	He's already started to write a second book, too.
I heard something funny from a friend yesterday.	He's donating all that money to charity as well.

B **PAIR WORK** Choose a story from the Vocabulary section and tell your partner about it. Add information to give more details.

Example:

A: I saw something interesting on TV last night. This woman found her long-lost twin sister. They were separated at birth. Also, the amazing thing is— they were living in the same city!

4 | Pronunciation Reduced vowel sounds

CD1 **41** **A** Listen and practice. Notice how vowel sounds are often reduced to /ə/ in unstressed syllables.

    /ə/   /ə/   /ə/   /ə/
1. broken   2. today   3. agree   4. woman

CD1 **42** **B** Listen and underline the reduced vowel sounds. Then practice saying the words.

1. children   2. local   3. second   4. cancel

ONLINE PRACTICE

SPEAK *with* CONFIDENCE

A **PAIR WORK** Choose one of these news stories. What do you think happened next? Prepare the next few lines of the story.

NEWS

Singer cancels tour
Isabel Perez has canceled her world tour. The popular pop star…

Teen starts college
Fifteen-year-old Raj Gupta has started his first year at Harvard University. He…

Grandmother breaks record
Eighty-year-old Millie West has broken a world record. Millie…

Actor saves life
A famous TV actor is a real-life hero after he saved the life of a child. Tony Lee…

B **GROUP WORK** Join another pair. Take turns telling your stories. Ask follow-up questions.

16 When did they release it?

- Asking when things happened
....
- Stating when things happened

1 | Vocabulary

A Match the current events to the examples.

_____ 1. a sporting success   a. Barack Obama was elected U.S. president in 2008.

_____ 2. a political change   b. China hosted the Olympic Games in 2008.

_____ 3. a key discovery   c. In 1922, Howard Carter found the tomb of King Tut.

_____ 4. a royal wedding   d. A tsunami struck in the Indian Ocean in December, 2004.

_____ 5. a celebrity scandal   e. Prince William married Kate Middleton on April 29, 2011.

_____ 6. a natural disaster   f. In 2001, actress Winona Ryder was arrested for shoplifting.

_____ 7. a daring rescue   g. In Chile, all 33 of the miners who were trapped underground were brought to the surface in October, 2010.

B **PAIR WORK** Tell your partner what you think was the top news story last year.

2 | Conversation

CD1 **43** **A** **Listen. When was the first _Harry Potter_ film released? How many questions did Glen get correct?**

 Glen: I'm ready for Friday's current events quiz. _____

 Allie: So, let me quiz you. When did Spain beat the Netherlands at the World Cup finals? _____

 Glen: That's easy. It was in 2012. Next question. _____

 Allie: Sorry. It was in 2010. Let's move on to entertainment. When was the first _Harry Potter_ film released?

 Glen: I think the first one was in 2008. _____
(2つ)

 Allie: Actually, it was in 2001. You'd better start studying!

B **PAIR WORK** Practice the conversation. Then find the best places to add the sentences below to the conversation and practice it again.

1. Just the year is OK.	3. It'll be a piece of cake!
2. Give me something harder.	4. Yeah—I'm sure it's correct.

pair with **VOCABULARY WORKSHEET 16**

3 | Language Booster

A Notice the different ways we ask and state when things happened.

Asking when things happened	Stating when things happened
When did China host the Olympics?	It was in 2008.
In what year did Apple release the iPad?	They released it in 2010.
Do you know when Prince William and Kate Middleton got married?	They got married on April 29, 2011.

B PAIR WORK Cover the second column in part A. Take turns asking and stating when things happened.

Example:

A: In what year did China host the Olympics?

B: It was in 2008.

4 | Listening

A Walter is a contestant on a game show. Look at the questions and possible answers. Guess the answers before you listen. Underline your guesses.

1. When did the Titanic sink?
    _____ a. April 15, 1912   _____ b. April 15, 1922   _____ c. April 15, 1932

2. Who hosted the Olympics in 1988?
    _____ a. South Korea   _____ b. Spain   _____ c. the United States

3. When did man first land on the moon?
    _____ a. July 20, 1959   _____ b. July 20, 1969   _____ c. July 20, 1979

4. In what decade was the first 3D movie?
    _____ a. the 1920s   _____ b. the 1950s   _____ c. the 1970s

CD1 **44 B** Listen. Check (✓) the correct answers. Did you beat Walter?

ONLINE PRACTICE

SPEAK *with* CONFIDENCE

A PAIR WORK Can you remember any news events for these categories in the past two years? Take turns asking and answering questions.

sports	entertainment	politics
weather	technology	local news

Our national soccer team won the regional championship last year.

B GROUP WORK Discuss what you remember about each news story. Answer any questions.

English in Action

ONLINE PRACTICE

1 | Preview

A PAIR WORK Look at the photos below. What do you think happens? Put them in order from 1 to 4.

2 | Practice

A Watch the video. Check your order in Preview. Did you guess correctly?

B Watch the video again. Fill in the blanks.

1. When Eric and Tom enter the apartment, the _____ is open.

2. Eric thinks they have been _____ while they were gone.

3. Tom calls the _____.

4. Eric's grandmother gave him _____.

5. Eric's missing object was under _____.

3 | Discuss

GROUP WORK Answer the questions.

1. Do you still have anything special from your childhood?
2. What is the most valuable thing you own?

CONFIDENCE BOOSTER

Student A: Turn to page 85.
Student B: Turn to page 93.

13 I used to play hopscotch.

A Student A: Ask Student B to tell you two things he or she used to enjoy doing as a child. Ask follow-up questions.

Student B: Tell Student A about two things you enjoyed when you were a child.

B Now change roles.

I can ask about childhood.
☐ Very well ☐ I need more practice.

I can reminisce about childhood.
☐ Very well ☐ I need more practice.
See Language Booster page 33.

14 She said she was sorry.

Student A and Student B: What were the last three things a friend said to you? Try to remember. Take turns reporting what he or she said. Ask follow-up questions.

I can report what someone said.
☐ Very well ☐ I need more practice.

See Language Booster page 35.

15 I read an unusual story.

Student A and Student B: Take turns talking about something you've heard in the news recently. Be sure to add information to make the story interesting.

I can talk about news.
☐ Very well ☐ I need more practice.

I can add information.
☐ Very well ☐ I need more practice.
See Language Booster page 37.

16 When did they release it?

A Student A: Ask Student B three questions. Ask when key events happened in his or her life.

Student B: Answer Student A's questions.

B Now change roles.

I can ask when things happened.
☐ Very well ☐ I need more practice.

I can state when things happened.
☐ Very well ☐ I need more practice.
See Language Booster page 39.

STORIES

13

14

15

16

REVIEW

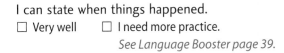
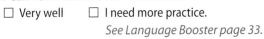

17 You didn't know?

1 | Vocabulary

A Match the types of friends with the correct definitions.

_____ 1. an old friend

_____ 2. an acquaintance

_____ 3. a best friend

_____ 4. a former friend

_____ 5. a lifelong friend

_____ 6. a childhood friend

_____ 7. a fair-weather friend

a. your number one friend

b. someone you know, but you don't consider a friend

c. a friend you had since you were a little kid

d. a friend that you've known for a long time

e. someone who was a friend, but isn't anymore

f. someone you are friends with for a lifetime

g. a friend who is nice only when he or she needs something

B **PAIR WORK** Tell your partner what you think the best type of friend is and the worst type of friend.

2 | Conversation

CD2 **02** **A** Listen. Why does Kal call Winnie? Where did Winnie see Brad?

Kal: Hi, it's Kal. Do you have a minute? It's about my best friend Brad.

Winnie: Sure. Is everything OK?

Kal: Yeah. I just feel like we're acquaintances these days.

Winnie: You do? Why?

Kal: He doesn't really call or text me much anymore. His mind seems to be somewhere else, too. The other day—

Winnie: Sorry, but can I interrupt for a second?

Kal: Of course.

Winnie: I think Brad got a part-time job.

Kal: He did?

Winnie: Yeah. I saw him at the coffee shop the other day, but he was working there!

Kal: Oh, I should really be a better friend!

B **PAIR WORK** Practice the conversation.

CD2 **03** **C** Listen. Write the three extra sentences you hear in the conversation. Practice the new conversation.

pair with VOCABULARY WORKSHEET 17

3 | Language Booster

A Notice the different ways we react with reply questions to express surprise or interest.

Comment	Reacting with reply questions
Brad is really busy these days.	He is?
Becky isn't having fun.	She isn't?
I feel like we're acquaintances.	You do?
Brad doesn't call me.	He doesn't?
I called you last night.	You did?
They didn't see each other.	They didn't?

B PAIR WORK Take turns completing these sentences and reacting with reply questions.

My close friends and I like to…   I once told an old friend…   I've known my best friend for…

4 | Pronunciation Using intonation in reply questions

CD2 **04** **A Listen and practice. Notice how intonation rises to show surprise and interest.**

A: My parents are best friends.

B: They are?

A: I used to watch a lot of movies.

B: You did?

B Circle the words to make the sentences true for you.

1. I would *answer the phone / ignore the call* if a friend called me at 3 a.m.

2. I feel it's *fine / silly / dangerous* to have a lot of friends.

3. It's good to have *one good friend / a few close friends / lots of friends.*

C GROUP WORK Share your answers. Others react with reply questions. Pay attention to the intonation.

ONLINE PRACTICE

SPEAK with CONFIDENCE

A Look at the questions below. Think about two close friends you have.

How long have you known them?   How are you alike and different?

How did you meet?   How has your friendship changed over time?

B GROUP WORK Talk about your friends. Ask questions to get more information.

18 A good friend is loyal.

1 | Vocabulary

A Complete the sentences with the correct words.

A good friend is...

1. _____ of your goals and dreams.

2. _____ and will stick with you in good times and in bad.

3. _____ and is always honest even when the truth hurts.

4. _____ and will never judge your actions.

5. _____ when you make a mistake or do something wrong.

6. _____ and takes an interest in you and your happiness.

7. _____ and someone who will always be there for you.

accepting
forgiving ✓
loyal ✓
reliable
truthful ✓
supportive ✓
caring

B PAIR WORK Tell your partner if you think you have the qualities above.

2 | Conversation

CD2 **05** **A** Listen. What kind of friends does Hugh like? What's important for Jo?

Jo: Have you made many friends since you moved here, Hugh?_____

Hugh: I've actually made quite a few friends. _____

Jo: What sort of people do you like to be friends with? _____

Hugh: To me, it's important for a friend to be truthful. You know—
they don't say things behind your back and stuff. _____

Jo: Also, an important thing is that they're reliable. Good friends are
always there when you need them, even if you don't see them often.

Hugh: I know what you mean.

B PAIR WORK Practice the conversation. Then find the best places to add the sentences below to the conversation and practice it again.

1. That's important to me.   3. Making new friends can be difficult.

2. I joined a school club.   4. What's important to you?

44   *pair with* VOCABULARY WORKSHEET 18

3 | Language Booster

A Notice the different ways we talk about what's important.

Asking about what's important	Describing what's important
What's important to you?	To me a friend needs to be reliable. It's important for a friend to be reliable.
What is the most important quality a friend should have?	The most important thing is how truthful someone is.

B **PAIR WORK** Take turns asking about and describing the qualities you think are the most important for a friend to have.

4 | Listening

CD2 **06** **A** Listen to four people talking about friends. Mark the statements T (true) or F (false).

_____ 1. The woman said she's already paid the money back to her friend.

_____ 2. The man's friend, Casey, agrees that his sister was acting silly. [ˈsɪli] a 傻的. 愚蠢的

_____ 3. The woman was upset because her friends wouldn't help her with homework.

_____ 4. The man became angry at his friend Patrick for something he did.

CD2 **06** **B** Listen again. Read the proverbs below from around the world. Which would be appropriate to say to each person? Write the letter of the best proverb for each conversation.

1. _____   2. _____   3. _____   4. _____

a. Only your real friends will tell you when your face is dirty. (Italy)

b. Before borrowing money from a friend, decide which you need most. (U.S.A.)

c. Hold a true friend with both of your hands. (Nigeria)

d. There are plenty of acquaintances in the world, but very few real friends. (China)

ONLINE PRACTICE

SPEAK with CONFIDENCE

A Think about three important qualities each of the following people should have.

a roommate	a parent
a language partner	a teacher
a boss	an employee

B **GROUP WORK** Share your ideas with two people. Do you agree?

19 I could do that.

1 | Vocabulary

A Look at these ways to make new friends. Write G (good idea) or B (bad idea).

_____ take a class   _____ join a student club   _____ make friends through friends

_____ play sports   _____ go to social events   _____ introduce yourself to people

_____ do volunteer work   _____ use social networks   _____ join an online group

B **PAIR WORK** Tell your partner what you think is the best way to make friends and why.

Example:

A: The best way to make friends is to take a class. Then you meet people with similar interests.

B: That sounds like a great idea.

2 | Conversation

CD2 **07** **A** Listen. Why doesn't Rod like Carrie's first suggestion? Why doesn't he like her second suggestion?

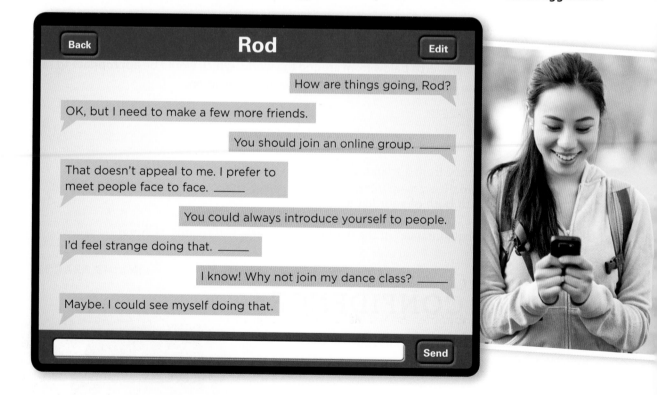

Rod

Back   Edit

> How are things going, Rod?

OK, but I need to make a few more friends.

> You should join an online group. _____

That doesn't appeal to me. I prefer to meet people face to face. _____

> You could always introduce yourself to people.

I'd feel strange doing that. _____

> I know! Why not join my dance class? _____

Maybe. I could see myself doing that.

Send

B **PAIR WORK** Practice the conversation. Then find the best places to add the sentences below to the conversation and practice the conversation again.

1. We're learning Tango right now.   3. I do that all the time.

2. I'm kind of shy, you know.   4. You never know who you're talking to online.

3 | Language Booster

A Notice the different ways we comment positively and negatively to suggestions.

Suggestion	Commenting positively	Commenting negatively
If you want to make friends, you should join an online group.	I might find that interesting. That sounds like it could be fun. I think I could do that. I could see myself doing that.	That doesn't really appeal to me. That doesn't sound like it would be fun. I'd feel strange doing that. I wouldn't feel comfortable doing that.

B **PAIR WORK** Take turns suggesting ways to make friends. Use the ideas in the Vocabulary section and your own ideas.

Example:

A: You should join a social network.

B: That doesn't really appeal to me.

4 | Listening

CD2 08 **A** Listen. Abigail is asking five people for suggestions on how to make friends. Write the suggestions.

Suggestion	Positively	Negatively
1.		
2.		
3.		
4.		
5.		

CD2 08 **B** Listen again. Does Abigail comment positively or negatively to each suggestion? Check (✓) the correct column.

ONLINE PRACTICE

SPEAK *with* CONFIDENCE

A How do you maintain your friendships? Make a list of things you can do to keep friendships strong. Use these or your own ideas.

Give friends small gifts.	Ask questions, but don't be nosy.
Listen to their problems.	Keep in touch regularly.
Remember their birthdays.	Never talk behind their back.

B **GROUP WORK** Share your ideas. Comment on the suggestions. Do you have many of the same ideas?

20 I wish I'd remembered.

• **Expressing regrets**

• **Offering solutions to problems**

1 | Vocabulary

A Sometimes we have small disagreements with friends or do things we later regret. Look at the possible solutions. Complete the sentences with the correct words.

feelings	involved	ignore	joke	apologize	problem

1. _____, even if you don't mean it.

2. Ask someone else to get _____.

3. _____ it and move on.

4. Be open about your _____.

5. Discuss the _____ with them.

6. Make a _____ about it.

B PAIR WORK Tell your partner how you feel about the ideas above.

Example:

A: I think it's good to apologize, but you have to mean it.

B: I agree. An apology has to be sincere.

2 | Conversation

CD2 **09** **A** Listen. Why did Brett forget the party? What does Dana suggest?

Brett: You'll never guess what happened. My friend John invited me to a party at his house last night, and I totally forgot about it.

Dana: Oh, no. How come?

Brett: I was so busy all week that it completely slipped my mind. I wish I'd remembered because it was his birthday.

Dana: Have you talked to him?

Brett: Not yet. I don't know what to do.

Dana: What you could do is call John now and apologize. I always say honesty is the best policy.

Brett: That's a good idea.

B PAIR WORK Practice the conversation.

CD2 **10** **C** Listen. Write the three extra sentences you hear in the conversation. Practice the new conversation.

pair with **VOCABULARY WORKSHEET 20**

3 | Language Booster

A Notice the different ways we express regrets and offer solutions to problems.

Expressing regrets		Offering solutions to problems	
I wish I had remembered I wish I hadn't forgotten about	my friend's birthday.	One thing you can do is What you could do is	call him and apologize.
I should have put a reminder	in my phone. on my calendar.	Something you might try is writing appointments down.	

B PAIR WORK Take turns expressing regrets about the situations below and offering solutions.

1. Your friend arrived late for an appointment and you told her how angry you were.

2. You borrowed money from a friend and forgot to return it until he reminded you.

3. You disagreed with your friend about something and had an argument about it.

4. Your friend is upset because you told her you didn't like the dress she was wearing.

4 | Pronunciation Linking of same consonant sounds

CD2 ⑪ **A** Listen and practice. Notice how the same consonant sound at the end of one word and at the beginning of the next word is pronounced only once.

1. What you could do is call John now and apologize.

2. I suppose Sandy could call later.

CD2 ⑫ **B** Listen. Then practice these conversations. Pay attention to the linking of same consonant sounds.

A: Does Sue know?
B: I suppose so.

A: I wish I could call Luke tonight.
B: You could talk to him Monday.

ONLINE PRACTICE

SPEAK *with* CONFIDENCE

GROUP WORK Look at what these people did. Discuss if they did the right thing. Give reasons for your opinion.

Bob lent his car to his friend Julia and when she returned it, Bob noticed some scratches on it. He was annoyed and asked his friend to pay for it. A few days later, his mom apologized for scratching the car while she was parking it.

Tim heard that his friend Matt had said something bad about him. He confronted Matt about it and found out that it was completely untrue.

English in Action

ONLINE PRACTICE

1 | Preview

PAIR WORK Look at the photo below. Eric, Jill, and Maria forgot Tom's birthday. What should they do?

2 | Practice

A Watch the video. Mark the statements T (true) or F (false).

_____ 1. Tom isn't answering his friends' calls. _____

_____ 2. Today is Tom's birthday. _____

_____ 3. Tom always says birthdays are his favorite days. _____

_____ 4. Eric suggests they don't do anything. _____

_____ 5. They buy Tom cookies for his birthday. _____

B Watch the video again. Rewrite the false statements to make them true.

3 | Discuss

GROUP WORK Answer the questions.

1. How do you like to celebrate your birthday? What do you usually do?
2. Have you ever forgotten someone's special day? What did you do?
3. Have you ever been to a surprise party? What was the event?

FRIENDS

17

18

19

20

VIDEO

CONFIDENCE BOOSTER Student A: Turn to page 86.
Student B: Turn to page 94.

17 You didn't know?

A **Student A:** Choose one friend and talk about him or her. Tell Student B how you met, how long you've been friends, and what you like to do together.

Student B: Listen to Student A. React with reply questions and follow-up questions.

B Now change roles.

I can react with reply questions.
☐ Very well   ☐ I need more practice.

See Language Booster page 43.

18 A good friend is loyal.

Student A and Student B: Ask and answer questions about what is important to be a good friend.

I can ask about what's important.
☐ Very well   ☐ I need more practice.

I can describe what's important.
☐ Very well   ☐ I need more practice.

See Language Booster page 45.

19 I could do that.

A **Student A:** Suggest to Student B two ways of achieving one of these things.

| have less stress | make extra money |

Student B: Listen to Student A's suggestions and comment positively or negatively.

B Now change roles. Student B chooses the other thing.

I can comment positively.
☐ Very well   ☐ I need more practice.

I can comment negatively.
☐ Very well   ☐ I need more practice.

See Language Booster page 47.

20 I wish I'd remembered.

A **Student A:** Tell Student B about something you regret saying or doing to a friend or family member.

Student B: Offer two possible solutions to Student A.

B Now change roles.

I can express regrets.
☐ Very well   ☐ I need more practice.

I can offer solutions to a problem.
☐ Very well   ☐ I need more practice.

See Language Booster page 49.

ONLINE PRACTICE

21 I'd rather not say.

• **Describing qualifications**

• **Avoiding answering**

1 | Vocabulary

A Which of these things do you think are important for getting a job today? Mark them
VI (very important), SI (somewhat important), or NI (not important).

_____ leadership _____ overseas experience _____ communication skills

_____ computer skills _____ good school grades _____ knowledge of current affairs

_____ work experience _____ a graduate degree _____ fluency in English

B **PAIR WORK** Tell your partner the skills you have and the ones you need.

Example:

A: I have good school grades, but I need to improve my computer skills.

2 | Conversation

CD2 ⑬ **A** Listen. Emily is applying for a marketing position. Why does she think she is suitable for the job?
What question doesn't she answer?

Interviewer: So tell me, why do you want to work in marketing?

Emily: Well, I took two courses in marketing at college and really enjoyed them. _____

Interviewer: I see. What skills do you have that would be useful for a career in marketing?

Emily: I developed communication and leadership skills
while working at *Mesa Design* for three months.

Interviewer: I see that here. Why only three months? _____

Emily: Um, I'd rather not say. I'll just say it wasn't the
right company for me. _____

Interviewer: All right. How are your computer skills?

Emily: Excellent. I can use all the main programs and
I taught myself web design. _____

B **PAIR WORK** Practice the conversation. Then find the best places to add the sentences below to the
conversation and practice it again.

1. Was there a problem?	3. But it was a positive experience.
2. After that, I wanted to pursue a job in marketing.	4. I'm a fast learner.

52 *pair with* VOCABULARY WORKSHEET 21

3 | Language Booster

A Notice the different ways we describe qualifications and avoid answering questions.

Describing qualifications	Avoiding answering
My communication skills are good.	I prefer not to say.
I can use all the main programs.	I'd rather not say.
People say I'd be good at marketing.	I'd rather not answer that.

B **PAIR WORK** Take turns completing these sentences.

| I'm good at… | My communication skills are… | People say I'd be a good… |

4 | Listening

CD2 **14** **A** Listen to Doug interviewing for a job as a hotel clerk. Number the questions from 1 to 6 in the order you hear them.

_____ a. How would someone describe you? _____

_____ b. What are your salary expectations? _____

_____ c. What is your greatest weakness? _____

_____ d. Are you OK working the night shift? _____

_____ e. What are some things you are good at? _____

_____ f. Why are you interested in this job? _____

CD2 **14** **B** Listen again. How does Doug answer the questions? Write notes above. Put an X after the question Doug avoids answering.

ONLINE PRACTICE

SPEAK *with* CONFIDENCE

A Look at these possible interview questions. Think of two more.

| Why are you interested in this job? | What are some things you are good at? | What are your qualifications? |

B **PAIR WORK** Imagine you have a job interview for one of these jobs. Practice for your interview. Take turns asking and answering the questions. Don't answer any questions you don't want to.

WANT ADS

Make coffee as a part time **Barista**. Part-time evening shift at hip student coffee shop near campus. Hourly wage and tips. Free coffee.

Tutor children in math and English at a local school. Work from 4 to 6, three days a week. Good school grades necessary. Salary negotiable.

22 It could be an ad for...

- Asking about probability and possibility
- Describing probability and possibility

1 | Vocabulary

A Look at the products or services. Try to match them to their slogans.

___f___ 1. fast food   a. The happiest place on earth.

_____ 2. online travel service   b. Because you're worth it.

_____ 3. soft drink   c. Leave the driving to us.

_____ 4. office supplies   d. Obey your thirst.

_____ 5. bus line   e. Lowest price guaranteed.

_____ 6. amusement park   f. Have it your way.

_____ 7. hair coloring   g. Taking care of business.

B PAIR WORK Tell your partner any advertising slogans you know.

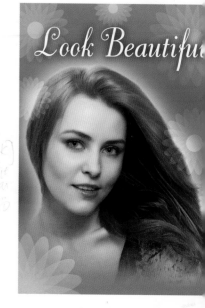

2 | Conversation

CD2 **15** **A** Listen. What does John think the ad is for? What does Amanda say makes an effective ad?

John: What do you think this ad could be for?

Amanda: I'm not sure. It looks like it could be for shampoo.

John: Shampoo? Maybe. I think it's probably for hair coloring.

Amanda: That's possible. Or I wonder if it's advertising cosmetics.

John: Whatever it is, I don't think it's very effective. It needs to be more clear. What do you think makes a good advertisement?

Amanda: Ads don't need to say much to be effective. They need to be simple and direct.

B PAIR WORK Practice the conversation.

CD2 **16** **C** Listen. Write the three extra sentences you hear in the conversation. Practice the new conversation.

3|Language Booster

A Notice the different ways we ask about and describe probability and possibility.

Asking about probability and possibility	Describing probability and possibility
What do you think this ad could be for? What do you think this ad is probably for? What do you suppose this ad is for?	It must be It looks like it could be I suppose it could be an ad for shampoo. I wonder if it's

B **PAIR WORK** Look at the ad slogans below. Take turns guessing what they are for.

> It's everywhere you want to be.   Connecting people.   Finger lickin' good.

Example:

A: I suppose the first one could be for phone service.

B: That's possible, but I wonder if it's for a credit card.

4|Pronunciation Unreleased consonants

CD2 **17** **A** Listen and practice. Notice how the final sounds /t/, /d/, /p/, /b/, /k/, and /g/ are not fully pronounced before other consonant sounds.

1. credi**t** card
2. taxica**b** company
3. foo**d** court
4. sil**k** jacket
5. chea**p** clothes
6. do**g** food

B **PAIR WORK** Take turns practicing this conversation. Pay attention to the unreleased consonants.

A: Wha**t** do you thin**k** this is?

B: I**t** could be for shampoo, bu**t** I think i**t** mus**t** be for skin cream.

ONLINE PRACTICE

SPEAK *with* CONFIDENCE

A **PAIR WORK** Make up a new slogan for a product. Use the ideas from the Vocabulary section, these ideas, or your own ideas.

fruit juice	athletic shoes	a computer
an automobile	an airline	a cell phone

B **CLASS ACTIVITY** Take turns reading your slogans. Can others guess what products you are advertising?

C **CLASS ACTIVITY** Vote on the best three slogans.

> Our slogan is "Start your day the natural way."

> I think it might be for yogurt.

23 The main reason is...

• Describing trends

• Giving reasons

1 | Vocabulary

A Look at these businesses. Match them to ways they could attract more customers. More than one answer is possible.

_____ 1. shopping malls   a. stay open 24 hours

_____ 2. banks   b. have fashion shows

_____ 3. convenience stores   c. reduce fees

_____ 4. language schools   d. have a lounge for socializing

_____ 5. supermarkets   e. sell 2-for-1 fares

_____ 6. airlines   f. offer free food samples

B PAIR WORK Compare your answers with a partner. Then give your own ideas.

2 | Conversation

CD2 **18** **A** Listen. Why are fewer people buying books at Phil's bookstore? What changes has he made?

Jan: How's the store doing, Phil?

Phil: Well, I've made some changes. People are buying fewer and fewer books from bookstores these days.

Jan: But why is that?

Phil: The main reason is that it's so easy to shop online and buy e-books.

Jan: So, what chçanges have you made?

Phil: We are bringing in authors for book signings.

Jan: That's a great idea!

Phil: People like to meet authors and hear them read.

Jan: That's true. People can't do that online.

Phil: Yes. And we've just opened this coffee shop.

B PAIR WORK Practice the conversation.

CD2 **19** **C** Listen. Write the three extra sentences you hear in the conversation. Practice the new conversation.

3 | Language Booster

A Notice the different ways we describe trends and give reasons.

Describing trends	Giving reasons	
More and more bookstores are closing.	It's due to fact that	it's so easy to shop online.
People are buying fewer and fewer books from bookstores these days.	The main reason is that	
People don't read as much as they used to.	One reason may be because	

B **PAIR WORK** Take turns describing trends and giving reasons. Use the businesses in the Vocabulary section.

Example:

A: More and more language schools have social events.

B: One reason may be because socializing helps students gain confidence.

4 | Pronunciation   Linking with /w/ and /y/

CD2 **20** **A** Listen and practice. Notice how some vowel sounds are linked with a /w/ or /y/ sound.

1. How/w/ is your bookstore doing?

2. We try/y/ and bring in authors.

3. Say, let's go/w/ and have a cup of coffee.

4. As we/y/ all know, people are buying fewer books.

CD2 **21** **B** Listen. Write the correct linked sound below: /w/ or /y/.

Do you know/   /if Bree/   /is going to go/   /and buy/   /a book before class?

ONLINE PRACTICE

SPEAK *with* CONFIDENCE

A **GROUP WORK** Think of trends that are affecting the things below. Give reasons for each trend in your country.

- shopping
- education
- employment
- transportation
- pop culture
- leisure time

> I think more and more people are shopping online.
>
> I agree. I think it's because it's more convenient to shop online.
>
> Another reason is that some people want to avoid the crowds at shopping malls.

B **CLASS ACTIVITY** Share your ideas. Do you agree on the trends and reasons?

It needs a good location.

1 | Vocabulary

A Look at the customer review about a clothing store. Complete the sentences with the words in the box.

logo	service	prices	idea	location	marketing

⭐⭐⭐⭐⭐

The _____ next to the train station is very convenient. All the employees were helpful and the _____ was great. The _____ are also affordable. Nothing is too expensive. Oh, and I really liked the _____. It's simple, but cool. The store recently did creative social network _____. It was a good _____. I would definitely go again!

Email ✉ Bookmark 🔖 Share this link ➕   Was this review ... ? [Helpful] [Amusing] [Not Helpful]

B PAIR WORK Tell your partner about two successful businesses in your city and why you think they are successful.

2 | Conversation

CD2 22 A Listen. What things does Carmen think are important for starting a café? What doesn't she think is important?

Carmen: I really want to open my own café. _____

Greg: What do you need to run a successful café?

Carmen: It needs a good location, like near a school, so I can get business from students. _____

Greg: That's a good idea. Is it necessary to have low prices?

Carmen: Definitely. The prices have to be affordable. It must have free wireless Internet, too. _____

Greg: Do you think you might need a more original idea?

Carmen: No, I just need to sell quality coffee.

Greg: I hope you're right. So, what are you going to name it?

Carmen: Name? I haven't thought of one. _____

B PAIR WORK Practice the conversation. Then find the best places to add the sentences below to the conversation and practice it again.

1. They're always hungry!   3. I think I'd be really good at it.

2. Let's try to think of one now.   4. I want customers to feel relaxed.

3 | Language Booster

A Notice the different ways we ask about and describe what's necessary.

Asking about what's necessary	Describing what's necessary
What do you need to run a successful café?	It needs a good location.
Is it necessary to have low prices?	The prices have to be affordable.
What else do you have to have?	It must have free wifi.

B **PAIR WORK** Ask and answer questions about what is necessary to run these businesses successfully.

a hair salon   an Internet café   a used bookstore

4 | Listening

CD2 23 **A** Listen to the beginning of an interview with a TV talk show host and the author of the book *Running a Small Business*. Mark the statements T (true) or F (false).

_____ 1. Every business is different.

_____ 2. Location is important for every business.

_____ 3. Word of mouth can't make a restaurant in an inconvenient place a success.

_____ 4. Customer service and quality products are important for all businesses.

CD2 24 **B** Listen to the rest of the interview. What does every business need to do to be successful?

1. _____   2. _____   3. _____

ONLINE PRACTICE

SPEAK with CONFIDENCE

A **PAIR WORK** Imagine you want to open one of these businesses. What do you need to make it successful?

a flower shop
a boutique hotel
a language school
a clothing store

A successful flower shop needs friendly service.

Right. And the employees have to know a lot so they can answer questions.

B **GROUP WORK** Compare your plans with another pair. Are there additional things that you think are necessary in both plans?

English in Action

ONLINE PRACTICE

1 | Preview

PAIR WORK Look at the photo of Tom below. Discuss the questions.

1. How is Tom dressed? _____

2. Where do you think Tom is? _____

3. What do you think he's doing? _____

2 | Practice

A Watch the video. Did you guess correctly? Write the words that Tom uses to describe himself.

1. _____ 2. _____ 3. _____

B Watch the video again. Check (✓) the questions you hear.

1. ☐ What makes you different?   ☐ What makes a difference?

2. ☐ How are you reliable and trustworthy?   ☐ Are you reliable and trustworthy?

3. ☐ What are some of your weaknesses?   ☐ What is your greatest weakness?

4. ☐ What are your reasons?   ☐ What is the reason?

3 | Discuss

GROUP WORK Answer the questions.

1. Have you ever had an interview? What was it for?

2. How would you describe yourself?

3. What can you say about your past experiences?

CONFIDENCE BOOSTER   Student A: Turn to page 87.
Student B: Turn to page 95.

BUSINESS

21
22
23
24

VIDEO

Speak NOW

 21 **I'd rather not say.**

A Student A: Student B chooses a job to interview for.
Ask for qualifications.

Student B: Answer Student A's questions, but avoid answering
some of them.

B Now change roles. Student A chooses a different job.

I can describe qualifications.
☐ Very well   ☐ I need more practice.

I can avoid answering a question.
☐ Very well   ☐ I need more practice.

See Language Booster page 53.

22 **It could be an ad for...**

Student A and Student B: Take turns asking about and describing
what these slogans might advertise.

The ultimate driving machine.	Fly the friendly skies.
The best part of wakin' up.	Breakfast of champions.

I can ask about probability and possibility.
☐ Very well   ☐ I need more practice.

I can describe probability and possibility.
☐ Very well   ☐ I need more practice.

See Language Booster page 55.

23 **The main reason is...**

A Student A: Tell Student B about two recent trends in your
hometown. Suggest reasons for the trends.

Student B: Ask follow-up questions. Offer your own reasons.

B Now change roles.

I can describe trends.
☐ Very well   ☐ I need more practice.

I can give reasons.
☐ Very well   ☐ I need more practice.

See Language Booster page 57.

24 **It needs a good location.**

A Student A: Ask Student B what he or she thinks is necessary to run
two of the businesses below.

a clothing store   a bakery   a bookstore   a health food store

Student B: Answer Student A's questions. Give reasons.

B Now change roles.

I can ask about what's necessary.
☐ Very well   ☐ I need more practice.

I can describe what's necessary.
☐ Very well   ☐ I need more practice.

See Language Booster page 59.

BUSINESS

21

22

23

24

REVIEW

ONLINE PRACTICE

25

You're expected to...

1 | Vocabulary

A Complete the sentences with the correct words.

decline	accept	acknowledge	expected	shake	bow	pour

1. In Ghana, _____ everyone at a social event.

2. In Korea, don't _____ your own drinks in restaurants.

3. In Japan, _____ and _____ hands with a person you meet for the first time.

4. In China, _____ a gift the first time it's offered. _____ the gift the third time.

5. In India, you are _____ to stand up when an older person enters the room.

B PAIR WORK Tell your partner about two customs in your country.

2 | Conversation

CD2 25 **A** Listen. Dan is going to China for the first time. What customs does Sarah tell him about?

Dan: So, what are some of the things I need to know when I'm in China?

Sarah: OK. Well, you're supposed to take off your shoes before you enter someone's home.

Dan: OK. That's the same in Japan and Korea.

Sarah: That's right. And when you visit someone's home, it's the custom to bring a small gift.

Dan: OK.

Sarah: But in China, if someone gives you a gift, you're not supposed to open it right away.

Dan: Got it! Thanks for the tips!

B PAIR WORK Practice the conversation.

CD2 26 **C** Listen. Write the three extra sentences you hear in the conversation. Practice the new conversation.

3 | Language Booster

A Notice the different ways we talk about expectations.

Describing what is expected		Describing what is not expected	
You're expected		You're not expected	
You're supposed	to take off your shoes before	You're not supposed	to open a gift right away.
It's the custom	you enter someone's home.	It's not the custom	
It's polite		It's impolite	

B PAIR WORK Take turns describing expectations in the country you are in now.

Example:

A: It's the custom to open a gift when you receive one.

B: Right. And you're not expected to arrive on time to a party.

4 | Pronunciation: Thought groups

CD2 **27 A** Listen and practice. Notice how longer sentences are divided into thought groups. There may be a slight pause between them.

1. It's polite / to shake hands / when you meet someone / for the first time.

2. It's impolite / to open a gift / in front of the person / who gave it to you.

CD2 **28 B** Listen. Then practice the sentences. Pay attention to the thought groups.

1. You're expected / to greet / the oldest person / first.

2. It's the custom / to take a small gift / when you visit / someone's home.

[KASEAA]

ONLINE PRACTICE

SPEAK *with* CONFIDENCE

A GROUP WORK In groups of three or four, choose one of the events below. Make a list of customs you know for that event. Name the country where that custom is observed.

a graduation	a birthday	a funeral
a wedding	an engagement	a business meeting

B CLASS ACTIVITY Take turns presenting your information to the class. Answer any questions.

26 What does it mean?

- Asking what something means
- Saying what something means

1 | Vocabulary

A Match the words and phrases to make a correct proverb.

_____ 1. Diligence   a. begins at home. (Your first duty is to care for your family.)

_____ 2. Haste   b. makes waste. (Something done too quickly may be done carelessly.)

_____ 3. Charity   c. is bliss. (What you do not know causes no worry or sadness.)

_____ 4. Ignorance   d. is the mother of good fortune. (Hard work brings rewards.)

_____ 5. Knowledge   e. is the spice of life. (Doing different things makes life interesting.)

_____ 6. Variety   f. is its own reward. (Don't expect praise for acting in a correct way.)

_____ 7. Virtue   g. is power. (It can be an advantage to know something others don't.)

B PAIR WORK Take turns explaining the proverbs in your own words.

2 | Conversation

CD2 29 A Listen. What is Emma's favorite proverb? What does it mean?

Tomas: Do you have any favorite proverbs, Emma?

Emma: I really like *"Laughter is the best medicine."* _____

Tomas: What does it mean to you?

Emma: It reminds me to find humor during difficult times. _____

Tomas: What about *"Charity begins at home."* What do you think it means?

Emma: I think it means that the most important thing is to care for your own family. _____

Tomas: I'm trying to learn lots of proverbs, but it's taking me a long time. _____

Emma: Don't worry. *"Rome wasn't built in a day."*

B PAIR WORK Practice the conversation. Then find the best places to add the sentences below to the conversation and practice it again.

1. In other words, put family first.
2. It's hard to remember them all.
3. I try to live by those words.
4. People say laughing heals.

3 | Language Booster

A Notice the different ways we ask about and say what something means.

Asking what something means	Saying what something means	
Do you know what it means?	It means	laugh and you'll feel better.
What does it mean to you?	It could mean to	put family first.
Do you have any idea what it means?	I think it means	
What do you think it means?	It reminds me to find humor during difficult times.	

B **PAIR WORK** Take turns asking and saying what these proverbs mean.

Beauty is only skin deep.   Love is blind.   Every cloud has a silver lining.

Example:

A: I think the first proverb means that beauty is not important.

B: I think it also means…

4 | Listening

A **GROUP WORK** Look at these proverbs. What do you think they mean?

_____ a. Look before you leap.

_____ b. Easy come, easy go.

_____ c. Don't judge a book by its cover.

_____ d. Actions speak louder than words.

_____ e. Great minds think alike.

_____ f. Don't cry over spilled milk.

CD2 30 **B** Listen. Five people are discussing different situations. Which proverb would be appropriate to say to them? Number the proverbs in part A from 1 to 5. There's one extra.

ONLINE PRACTICE

SPEAK *with* CONFIDENCE

A **PAIR WORK** Write three interesting proverbs you know from your own culture or from another culture.

1. _____

2. _____

3. _____

B **GROUP WORK** Share your proverbs. Say what you think your classmates' proverbs mean.

28 It must have been...

• **Speculating with more certainty**

• **Speculating with less certainty**

1 | Vocabulary

A PAIR WORK Read the news stories below. Do you believe any of them? Why or why not?

NEWS STORIES

A **UFO** was spotted over the city by hundreds of people last night. A few eyewitnesses claimed they could see **aliens** in the window. The military refused to comment on the possibility of **aircraft** in the skies. Some say it was a lost weather **balloon**.

A large hairy **creature** was seen in a forest near campus last weekend. Local teen Alex Lim says it looked like a giant **bear**, but walked like a **gorilla.** Police suspect it's a man in a **costume** having some fun.

A woman claims she has a photograph of a **ghost.** Sally Corwin, 34, posted the photo on her website, showing a woman's face. Some say it's Sally's **reflection** although no mirror is present. Other say it's **smoke.** Most experts claim the photo is a **fake.**

B PAIR WORK Tell your partner if you've ever seen anything unusual.

2 | Conversation

CD2 33 A Listen. Does Nina think the lights were from a UFO? Why not?

Adam: Did you hear about those strange lights over the city on Sunday night?

Nina: No, I didn't.

Adam: Apparently, a lot of people saw bright lights moving across the sky. They thought the lights were from a UFO.

Nina: I doubt it. It must have been a plane.

Adam: Maybe, but there were lots of them, and they were moving around in circles.

Nina: It could have been a flock of birds. Birds move around in circles sometimes.

Adam: It couldn't have been birds. Birds don't have lights attached to them!

Nina: Whatever it was, it couldn't have been a UFO.

Adam: Why not?

Nina: Because there is no such thing!

B PAIR WORK Practice the conversation.

CD2 34 C Listen. Write the three extra sentences you hear in the conversation. Practice the new conversation.

3│Language Booster

A Notice the different ways we speculate about things.

Speculating with more certainty		Speculating with less certainty	
It must have been	a plane.	It may have been	
It couldn't have been	a UFO.	It could have been	a flock of birds.
		It might have been	

B PAIR WORK Take turns speculating on the events in the Vocabulary section.

Example:

A: The UFO could have been a weather balloon.

B: That's possible. Or it might have been a military aircraft.

A: I think eyewitnesses must have been frightened.

4│Pronunciation Reduction of past modals

CD2 **35** **A** Listen and practice. Notice how *have* is reduced in these sentences.

              've
1. You must have seen a plane.

                                 've
2. It couldn't have been a UFO.

B PAIR WORK Take turns speculating on the situation below. Pay attention to the reduction of *have*.

Situation:

Someone knocked on your door and shouted your name at 3 a.m. last night.

Speculations:

You must have fallen asleep.   There might have been an emergency.

The person may have lost his or her key.   It couldn't have been a robber.

ONLINE PRACTICE

SPEAK *with* CONFIDENCE

A PAIR WORK Discuss each of these situations. Speculate on what happened.

The sky is green one day.

You hear a voice calling your name, but no one is there.

You receive calls from the same unknown number, but no one speaks.

Your friend saw a large cat-like animal on the school roof.

B GROUP WORK Share your ideas. Can you agree on what happened?

English in Action

ONLINE PRACTICE

1 | Preview

PAIR WORK Look at the photo on the left. Maria is explaining the idiom, *"Jack of all trades, master of none."* Discuss and write what you think it means.

Jack of all trades

2 | Practice

A Watch the video. What does *"Jack of all trades, master of none"* mean?

_____

B Watch the video again. Complete the sentences below.

1. _____ got a job at an advertising company.

2. Jill is writing a _____.

3. In Japan and Korea you should take your _____ off when entering a house.

4. _____ explains the expression Jack of all trades, master of none.

5. Jill says Maria should be a _____.

3 | Discuss

GROUP WORK Answer the questions.

1. What custom from your country should Jill blog about?

2. What expression from your language do you think foreigners should know?

3. Could you explain it to them?

CULTURE

25

26

27

28

VIDEO

CONFIDENCE BOOSTER

Student A: Turn to page 88.
Student B: Turn to page 96.

25 You're expected to...

Student A and **Student B**: Discuss what is expected when you go to someone's home for dinner. What time do you arrive? What do you bring?

I can describe what is expected.
☐ Very well   ☐ I need more practice.

I can describe what is not expected.
☐ Very well   ☐ I need more practice.

See Language Booster page 63.

26 What does it mean?

A **Student A:** Ask Student B what one of the proverbs means.

Like father, like son.   Don't put all your eggs in one basket.

Student B: Answer Student A's questions.

B Now change roles. Student B chooses the other proverb.

I can ask what something means.
☐ Very well   ☐ I need more practice.

I can say what something means.
☐ Very well   ☐ I need more practice.

See Language Booster page 65.

27 What will happen if...?

Student A and **Student B**: Take turns asking about and describing superstitions that bring good and bad luck. Talk about lucky or unlucky numbers, days, or other ideas of your own.

I can ask about consequences.
☐ Very well   ☐ I need more practice.

I can describe consequences.
☐ Very well   ☐ I need more practice.

See Language Booster page 67.

28 It must have been...

A **Student A:** Choose one of the situations below. Then speculate with less certainty on the cause.

A woman claims she saw a shadow in her closet.

A man says he woke up one day and his furniture had been rearranged.

Student B: Listen to what Student A says. Then speculate with more certainty.

B Now change roles.

I can speculate with more certainty.
☐ Very well   ☐ I need more practice.

I can speculate with less certainty.
☐ Very well   ☐ I need more practice.

See Language Booster page 69.

ONLINE PRACTICE

Cars will most likely fly.

• **Making a probable prediction**

• **Making a definite prediction**

1 | Vocabulary

A Do you think these things will exist in 20 years? Mark ✓ (will exist) or ✗ (won't exist).

_____ cash   _____ printed books   _____ landline phones

_____ laptops   _____ credit cards   _____ gas-powered cars

_____ DVDs   _____ watches   _____ language teachers

B **PAIR WORK** Tell your partner what you think will exist or won't exist.

Example:

A: In 20 years, credit cards won't exist. It will all be digital.

2 | Conversation

CD2 **36** **A** Listen. What does the engineer say cars will be like in the future? What will be driving cars in the future?

 Katie: So, could you tell me what you think cars of the future will be like? _____

 Engineer: Well, they'll be faster and lighter. Cars will be made of plastic—a light and very strong plastic.

 Katie: Interesting. And what kind of fuels will they use? _____

 Engineer: They'll likely be using hydrogen. _____ They'll definitely be cleaner than today's cars. We're working on zero emission cars.

 Katie: That will be fantastic. Is it possible that cars may not need drivers?

Engineer: Oh, yes. One day, computers will make all the decisions for the driver and even control the driving. The driver will just sit back and relax. _____

B **PAIR WORK** Practice the conversation. Then find the best places to add the sentences below to the conversation and practice it again.

1. They definitely won't be using gasoline.   3. A driver could even sleep.

2. Will they still use gasoline?   4. How will they be different?

3 | Language Booster

A Notice the different ways we make predictions.

Making a probable prediction		Making a definite prediction	
Cars could		Tomorrow's cars will	
Cars will probably	be made of plastic.	Cars will definitely	be faster and lighter.
Cars will likely	fly.	Cars won't	use hydrogen.
Cars will most likely			

B **PAIR WORK** Take turns making predictions. Use the ideas from the Vocabulary section and your own ideas.

4 | Listening

CD2 **37** **A** Listen. A radio host is interviewing a futurologist. Check (✓) the things a futurologist does.

_____ 1. predicts the future

_____ 2. suggests the likelihood of things

_____ 3. studies the past and the present

_____ 4. looks at trends and patterns

_____ 5. looks at the short-term future

CD2 **38** **B** Listen to the rest of the interview. Does the futurologist think these things are probable or not probable? Check (✓) the correct column.

	Probable	Not probable
1. People will store their minds on a computer.		
2. There will be brain transplants.		
3. People will travel through time.		
4. Computers will have emotions.		
5. People will live forever.		

ONLINE PRACTICE

SPEAK *with* CONFIDENCE

A **PAIR WORK** Think of what could or will happen in these areas in the future. Agree on a prediction for each topic.

medicine	technology	transportation
food	weather	entertainment

I think there will be a cure for cancer.

Me too. When do you think it will happen?

B **GROUP WORK** Share your predictions. Do others agree with your predictions?

30 | That's a really good idea!

• Adding emphasis

1 | Vocabulary

A Some scientists believe the world's climate could increase by up to 5°C within the next 100 years. Circle the things below that you think will be affected by this climate change.

ice caps   storms   rainforests

sea levels   fresh water   cities

coral reefs   animal species

B **PAIR WORK** Tell your partner why you chose your answers.

Example:

A: If temperatures rise, the ice caps will melt.

B: And then sea levels will rise.

2 | Conversation

CD2 **39** **A** Listen. Why does Nicki think glass is better than plastic? What does Wes say about glass?

Wes: I read that they've banned plastic bottles in some European towns.

Nicki: That's a good idea.

Wes: Why do you say that?

Nicki: Well, if they ban plastic bottles, companies will have to make glass bottles.

Wes: Are you saying glass is better than plastic?

Nicki: Yes! Glass is much better than plastic.

Wes: But why?

Nicki: Because plastic breaks down so slowly. It stays on our planet for a long time.

Wes: But using more glass will also affect the environment. Making glass uses a lot of energy.

Nicki: I hadn't thought of that. To be honest, I don't know what the best solution is.

B **PAIR WORK** Practice the conversation.

CD2 **40** **C** Listen. Write the three extra sentences you hear in the conversation. Practice the new conversation.

3|Language Booster

A Notice the different ways we add emphasis.

Comment	Adding emphasis
Glass is more expensive.	Glass is definitely more expensive.
Glass is better than plastic.	Glass is much better than plastic.
That's a good idea.	That's a really good idea.
That's bad for the environment.	That's certainly bad for the environment.

B **PAIR WORK** Take turns adding emphasis to the sentences below.

The weather will change.	Storms will be stronger.
Ice caps may melt fast.	Sea levels will rise.

Example:

A: The weather will certainly change.

B: Yes, there will definitely be problems if it does.

4|Pronunciation Emphatic stress

CD2 **41** **A** Listen and practice. The first sentence in each pair already has added emphasis. You can emphasize this even more by adding strong stress.

1. Glass is definitely more expensive.   Glass is **definitely** more expensive.

2. Glass is much better than plastic.   Glass is **much** better than plastic.

B **PAIR WORK** Practice saying the sentences in the Language Booster section. Add emphatic stress.

ONLINE PRACTICE

SPEAK *with* CONFIDENCE

GROUP WORK Discuss these questions. Give your opinions.

Is the Earth getting warmer?

Will there be problems if the earth gets warmer?

How will cities be different in the future?

> The Earth is definitely getting warmer.
> It's going to be a really big problem.
> But I think it's warming up pretty slowly.
> Why do you say that?

I'll pick you up.

1 | Vocabulary

A PAIR WORK Look at these chores. Which word doesn't belong? Cross it out. Compare with a partner.

1. pick up   the clothes / my children / ~~the buildings~~

2. drop off   the counter / my friend / the dry-cleaning

3. clean out   the desk / the pencils / the closet

4. hang up   the clothes / the picture / the dishes

5. throw out   the yard / the papers / old food

6. wipe off   the counter / the garbage / the sink

7. put away   the dishes / the groceries / my children

8. take out   the garbage / the recycling / the counter

B PAIR WORK Tell your partner which chores you do often and which ones you never do.

2 | Conversation

CD2 **42** **A** Listen. Why are Dan and Mike having a party? How are Doug and Carlos going to get there?

Doug: Hey, Carlos. It's Doug. Do you have any plans later?

Carlos: Um, I guess. I plan to clean my room later. Why do you ask?

Doug: Dan and Mike are having a party tonight. Mike's leaving for the summer so it's kind of a goodbye party. Lots of our friends will be there.

Carlos: It sounds fun...

Doug: Yeah. So, can you make it?

Carlos: Sure. I'll hurry and get all this stuff done.

Doug: Great. I'll pick you up. My sister is going to lend me her car.

Carlos: Really?

Doug: Yeah. I'll be going right by your dorm. What time is good?

Carlos: Anytime.

Doug: OK. I'll come around 7 p.m.

B PAIR WORK Practice the conversation.

CD2 **43** **C** Listen. Write the three extra sentences you hear in the conversation. Practice the new conversation.

    pair with VOCABULARY WORKSHEET 31

3│Language Booster

A Notice the different ways we describe plans, and make decisions and promises.

Describing plans		Making decisions and promises
I plan to I'm going to I have to I'm planning to	clean my desk out later.	I'll pick you up. I'll come around 7:00. I'll call when I'm close.

B PAIR WORK Imagine you are going to do three of the things in the Vocabulary section. Take turns telling each other. Then decide what you will do together afterwards.

Example:

A: I have to drop off the dry-cleaning.

B: Can you watch a movie after?

A: I'll try to be quick.

4│Pronunciation   Stress in two-word verbs

CD2 44 **A** Listen and practice. Notice the stress in these two-word verbs.

1. **Clean out** my desk   **Clean** my desk **out**   **Clean** it **out**

2. **Throw out** papers   **Throw** papers **out**   **Throw** them **out**

B PAIR WORK Practice these sentences. Pay attention to stress.

1. I'll **take** the recycling **out**.   3. I'm planning to **clean** the closet **out**.

2. I'll **pick** you **up** later.   4. Are you going to **put away** the dishes?

ONLINE PRACTICE

SPEAK *with* CONFIDENCE

A Write down three things you're planning to do this Saturday and Sunday.

Saturday

1. _____

2. _____

3. _____

Sunday

4. _____

5. _____

6. _____

B GROUP WORK Share your plans. Then decide what to do together on one of the days. Decide where you'll go, how you'll get there, and any other details.

I'm going to the park at 2:00 on Saturday.

I'll be studying at the library then.

The weather is supposed to be beautiful! Can you guys come?

Yes! I'll bring some drinks and some snacks.

What do you hope to do?

1 | Vocabulary

A Look at these goals people sometimes set for themselves. Rank them from 1 (most important) to 10 (least important).

_____ be financially independent

_____ lose weight

_____ be more confident

_____ get out of debt

_____ get my own place

_____ go to graduate school

_____ move out of my parents' home

_____ manage money better

_____ get in better shape

B PAIR WORK Tell your partner which goals you think will be easy to achieve and hard to achieve.

2 | Conversation

CD2 45 **A** Listen. What doesn't Hung want to do after graduation? What does Nicole hope to do?

Nicole: So, do you have any plans after graduation? _____

Hung: I don't want to get a job right away. I feel like I need a break.
I'd like to take some time off and travel around Europe. _____

Nicole: How fun. Where do you want to go?

Hung: I'm not sure. I want to see Italy, Spain, and France.
I don't know if I can go to all three. _____

Nicole: They all sound great to me.

Hung: What about you?

Nicole: I want to find a job right away. Then I hope to
move out of my parents' home and get my own place.

Hung: I wish I could get my own place, too. _____

B PAIR WORK Practice the conversation. Then find the best places to add the sentences below to the conversation and practice it again.

1. Are you going to look for a job?   know that will have to wait.

2. I'll have to choose just one.   4. I'   dreamed of going there.

pair with **VOCABULARY WORKSHEET 32**

3 | Language Booster

A Notice the different ways we ask about and discuss goals and wishes.

Asking about goals and wishes	Discussing goals and wishes	
What are your goals?	I want to	
What would you like	I'd like to	do some traveling.
What do you hope	to do?	I hope to	get my own place.
What do you wish you could do?	I wish I could	

B **PAIR WORK** Ask and answer questions about goals and wishes using the ideas in the Vocabulary section or your own ideas.

Example:

A: What would you like to do?

B: I'd like to get my own place. Do you want to get your own place?

4 | Listening

CD2 **46** **A** Listen to four people discussing their goals and wishes. Number the pictures from 1 to 4.

CD2 **46** **B** Listen again. How do they plan to achieve their goals? Take notes.

1. _____   3. _____

2. _____   4. _____

C **PAIR WORK** Tell your partner if you have any of the same goals and how you might achieve them differently.

ONLINE PRACTICE

SPEAK *with* CONFIDENCE

A List three personal goals you would like to achieve.

Within the next year: _____

Within the next few years: _____

Within the next ten years: _____

B **GROUP WORK** Share your goals. Discuss the best ways to achieve them.

GOAL SETTING
S SPECIFIC
M MEASURABLE
A ATTAINABLE
R RELEVANT
T TIME-BOUND

English in Action

ONLINE PRACTICE

1 | Preview

PAIR WORK Eric, Tom, Jill, and Maria are talking about the future. The photos below represent their predictions for the future. Do you believe our future will look like any of these photos?

FUTURE

29

30

31

32

VIDEO

2 | Practice

A Watch the video. Number the photos above from 1 to 3 in the order you see them.

B Watch the video. Who says these things? Eric, Tom, Jill, or Maria? Write their names.

_____ 1. People won't use laptops because there will be large computer screens that look like TVs everywhere.

_____ 2. Cars will finally fly!

_____ 3. I think cars will run from energy in plants.

_____ 4. I think things will be just as they are now.

3 | Discuss

GROUP WORK Answer the questions.

1. Which of the items above do you think are most likely to happen?

2. What is one invention you hope we will have in the future?

CONFIDENCE BOOSTER

Student A: Turn to page 89.
Student B: Turn to page 97.

Speak NOW

29 **Cars will most likely fly.**

Student A and Student B: Take turns making predictions about the topics below.

| cities | mobile phones |
| TV | space travel |

I can make a probable prediction.
☐ Very well   ☐ I need more practice.

I can make a definite prediction.
☐ Very well   ☐ I need more practice.

See Language Booster page 73.

30 **That's a really good idea!**

A Student A: Complete these statements and tell Student B. Give your opinion and add emphasis when you feel strongly about something.

| Pollution is... | Climate change is... | The future of... |

Student B: Listen to Student A. Give your own opinion.

B Now change roles.

I can add emphasis.
☐ Very well   ☐ I need more practice.

See Language Booster page 75.

31 **I'll pick you up.**

Student A and Student B: Discuss your evening plans. Find a time to do something together. Agree on where you'll go, what you'll do, and how you'll meet.

I can describe plans.
☐ Very well   ☐ I need more practice.

I can make decisions and promises.
☐ Very well   ☐ I need more practice.

See Language Booster page 77.

32 **What do you hope to do?**

A Student A: Tell Student B about some of the personal goals you have set for yourself in the future and what you will do to achieve them.

Student B: Listen to Student A and ask follow-up questions.

B Now change roles.

I can ask about goals and wishes.
☐ Very well   ☐ I need more practice.

I can discuss goals and wishes.
☐ Very well   ☐ I need more practice.

See Language Booster page 79.

ONLINE PRACTICE

Student A
Do you need to be loyal?

1a. Two owners of a software company, Kevin and Kristy, chose the seven most important attributes for a new manager. Look at the information below. Ask Student B questions to fill in the blanks.

Example:

A: Does Kevin think the new manager needs to be a born leader?

B: No, he doesn't. Does Kristy think a manager needs to be a born leader?

A: Yes, she does.

Attributes	Kevin	Kristy		You	Your Partner
born leader	*no*	yes			
problem solver	yes				
optimist		no			
flexible	no				
mature	yes	yes			
reliable	yes				
responsible	yes				
honest		yes			
respectful		yes			
loyal		no			

1b. What attributes do you think a manager needs? Write yes in the chart above for your top five attributes. Compare your list with Student B's list. Give reasons for your choices.

Conversation Practice

2. Have a conversation with Student B (1–8). Read the first sentence to him or her. Listen to his or her response (2). If it is correct, choose the next correct response to continue the conversation.

1. Tell me more about your family.

3. a. How would you describe your parents?
   b. Does Dinos have a large extended family?

5. a. Excuse me, but may I interrupt? My family is just the opposite.
      My mother is quiet, and my father is talkative.
   b. Anyway, Marie is the first born, and she is married already.

7. a. She is engaged to a know-it-all.
   b. Wow! You have a large family. Where do you fall in the birth order?

Student A
What is the rule?

1. Look at the rules for student dorms. Ask Student B questions to fill in the blanks.

Example:

A: What is the rule about triple rooms?

B: All new students have triple rooms. What is the rule about fixing problems in the room?

A: All problems with the room must be reported to the dorm supervisor.

(Triple rooms) *All new students have triple rooms.*

Problems with the room must be reported to the dorm supervisor.

(Curfew)

Guests are not allowed after 11 p.m.

(The pool)

Problems with the bathroom must be reported to the front desk.

(Lost keys)

All valuables must be kept in locked closets.

Conversation Practice

2. Have a conversation with Student B (1–8). Read the first sentence to him or her. Listen to his or her response (2). If it is correct, choose the next correct response to continue the conversation.

1. Excuse me. There are some problems with my hotel room.

3. a. That won't be necessary.
   b. The toilet is not working and the window doesn't close.

5. a. No, it's not. I'd like a different room, please.
   b. No, the bus driver will take you around the city.

7. a. I'll get someone to bring you another towel.
   b. I prefer to keep my double room. Can you send someone, please?

Student A
What is the reason?

1a. Report the reasons for going to these places. Ask Student B questions to fill in the blanks.

Example:

A: Can you tell me why you have to go to the boutique?

B: The wedding planner said the dress was ready. Can you tell me why
you need to go to the hair salon?

A: My hairstylist says my hair is too long.

Person	Place	Reason
wedding planner	boutique	the dress is ready
hairstylist	hair salon	my hair is too long
	health food store	
computer technician	electronics store	repair my laptop because I have a virus
	dry cleaners	
student adviser	office supply store	buy a folder and notebook for each class

1b. Tell your partner how you feel about getting three of the things done from the list above. Use three of the words below.

| broke | sleepy | stressed | lonely | forgetful | sick | overwhelmed |

Conversation Practice

2. Have a conversation with Student B (1–8). Read the first sentence to him or her. Listen to his or her response (2). If it is correct, choose the next correct response to continue the conversation.

1. Hello. I'd like to join this gym.

3. a. Sure. One thing I should do is to cook at home more.
   b. Sure. I feel overwhelmed and stressed at work. I think exercise will help.

5. a. Yes. Here is my driver's license. Can you please tell me what the pool hours are?
   b. Please accept my apologies. I think I gave you the wrong phone number.

7. a. Thank you, but I'm afraid you misspelled my name on the card.
   b. I think you need to take bus number 27 if you want to go to the hair salon.

Student A
Nick used to play checkers.

1a. Look at the chart below. Ask and answer questions with *used to* and *used to be* to fill in the blanks.

Example:

A: Did Nick use to play checkers?

B: Yes, he did. Did Patty use to play hopscotch?

A: No, she didn't.

	Nick	Patty
play checkers	yes	yes
play hopscotch		no
go to the zoo		no
ride a bike around town		yes
donate toys to charity		yes
score goals in soccer		yes
catch balls		yes

1b. Tell Student B a story (you read, saw on TV, or heard from someone) that you think of when you see one of the words below. Respond to Student B's story with the words you think he or she is trying to talk about.

lucky	strange	awful	embarrassing	scary	disgusting	romantic

Example:

A: I remember when I was 12 years old, and it was the first day of school. When I got to my classroom, I tripped and fell down in front of the whole class.

B: How embarrassing!

Conversation Practice

2. Have a conversation with Student B (1–8). Read the first sentence to him or her. Listen to his or her response (2). If it is correct, choose the next correct response to continue the conversation.

1. When did your older brother become a doctor at Mercy Hospital?

3. a. Sure. I used to play hopscotch, but I don't anymore. How about you?
   b. I asked because my mother works there. She said she knows some new doctors there.

5. a. My mom works in the children's clinic.
   b. No he doesn't. He likes to play checkers, and he's writing his third book, too.

7. a. They must know each other. I heard it's a great place to work.
   b. I heard an interesting story last night on TV.

Student A
How does she know him?

1a. Pam has many kinds of friends. Ask Student B questions about her friends to help you fill in the blanks.

Example:

A: How does Pam know Craig?

B: They were World History classmates. What kind of friend is Craig?

A: He's a fair-weather friend to Pam.

Name	How They Know Each Other	Type of Person	Type of Friend
Craig	World History class	funny	fair-weather friend
Lily	volunteer work		
Yang		a good listener and tries to help solve problems	
Cindy	live next door		best friend

1b. Tell Student B about one of your friends. What is your friend's name? How did you meet? What type of friend and person is he or she?

Conversation Practice

2. Have a conversation with Student B (1–8). Read the first sentence to him or her. Listen to his or her response (2). If it is correct, choose the next correct response to continue the conversation.

1. I wanted to ask you a question. Do you have any cyber friends?

3. a. To me, a friend needs to be truthful, supportive, and caring. What do you think?
   b. I wouldn't say that I have a lot, but I do have some. I prefer meeting people face-to-face.

5. a. You do? Why do you think that is?
   b. One thing you can do is send her a small gift. Do you think she'll forgive you then?

7. a. You should join a club. That way you know you have the same interests.
   b. I think I could do that because that sounds interesting. Would you feel comfortable doing that?

Student A
What is the job?

1. **Look at the job advertisement. Ask Student B questions to fill in the blanks.**

Example:

A: What is the name of the language school?

B: Brighton English Language School. What kind of instructor are they looking for?

A: A full-time Italian instructor.

CONFIDENCE BOOSTER 21–24

___Brighton___   ___English___   **Language School**

Position:

Full-time Italian Instructor

Education and Experience:

Preferred graduate degree with three years of work experience

_____ work experience a plus

Responsibilities:

— teach 15 hours per week

— hold office hours _____ hours per week

— academic advising

Requirements and Abilities:

— _____ letter and resume

— three letters of recommendation or three academic contacts with telephone and e-mail

— fluent in English

— excellent _____ skills

— solid computer skills

Conversation Practice

2. **Have a conversation with Student B (1–8). Read the first sentence to him or her. Listen to his or her response (2). If it is correct, choose the next correct response to continue the conversation.**

1. Have you noticed that store owners are finding new and creative ways to attract customers these days?

3. a. It's a nice service. Shopping is easier without your children.
   b. People say I'm good at marketing because my communication skills are good.

5. a. Really? Have you ever tried a class?
   b. More and more bookstores are closing because people don't buy books these days.

Student A
How can we succeed?

1. This is a brochure for new students. Ask Student B questions to fill in the blanks.

Example:

A: What is the most important skill for success?

B: Diligence. What is power?

A: Knowledge is power.

New Student Success

_____ is the most important skill for success.

Follow the suggestions for success:

- Knowledge is power, so get as much as you can in your chosen field of study.

- _____ of the rules is no excuse for breaking them.

- Take a variety of courses in your first two years because you may find you prefer another major.

- Keep all assignment deadlines in a calendar.

- _____ to work hard.

Conversation Practice

2. Have a conversation with Student B (1–8). Read the first sentence to him or her. Listen to his or her response (2). If it is correct, choose the next correct response to continue the conversation.

1. I find learning about cultural traditions so interesting. Don't you?

3. a. I did know that. The same is true in a lot of countries, but in the United States, you wear your shoes indoors.
   b. It means you're supposed to take off your shoes before you enter someone's home.

5. a. Yes, I do. One thing to remember is you should shake the hand of everyone in the wedding party after the ceremony.
   b. No, I don't. It means you're expected to bow. Also, it's impolite to open a gift in front of the person who gave it to you.

7. a. It must have been a plane. It couldn't have been a UFO because there's no such thing.
   b. That's true, too. And you should buy a gift. You can send it in advance.

Student A
What will you do?

1a. This is a list of things Angelica wants to do in the future. Ask Student B questions to fill in the blanks.

Example:

A: What will Angelica do with the things she doesn't use?

B: She will throw them out. What will she manage better?

A: She will manage her money better.

Angelica's Checklist for the Future

Immediate Future

☐ _____ _____ the things I don't use

☐ manage my money better

☐ get in better shape by exercising regularly and losing weight

☐ buy a _____

☐ go to graduate school in a major city

Distant Future

☐ get a _____ job

☐ get _____

☐ have children

1b. Put a check (✓) next to three items from Angelica's list that you want to do in your future. Tell Student B the reasons for your choices.

Conversation Practice

2. Have a conversation with Student B (1–8). Read the first sentence to him or her. Listen to his or her response (2). If it is correct, choose the next correct response to continue the conversation.

1. What do you think you would like to do in the future?

3. a. That's a great idea! I can see you doing something like that. What do you wish you could change?
   b. I'm going to throw out old papers because recycling should absolutely be encouraged.

5. a. I want to do some errands, so I'll hurry and get all this stuff done fast. Then I'll come pick you up since I'll be going right by your dorm.
   b. That's a good idea, but I can't imagine cars using anything except gas.

Student B
Do you need to be loyal?

1a. Two owners of a software company, Kevin and Kristy, chose the seven most important attributes for a new manager. Look at the information below. Ask Student A questions to fill in the blanks.

Example:

A: Does Kevin think the new manager needs to be a born leader?

B: No, he doesn't. Does Kristy think a manager needs to be a born leader?

A: Yes, she does.

Attributes	Kevin	Kristy
born leader	no	yes
problem solver		yes
optimist	yes	
flexible	no	yes
mature	yes	
reliable		no
responsible		yes
honest	no	
respectful	yes	
loyal	yes	

You	Your Partner

1b. What attributes do you think a manager needs? Write yes in the chart above for your top five attributes. Compare your list with Student A's list. Give reasons for your choices.

Conversation Practice

2. Have a conversation with Student A (1–8). Listen to his or her sentence. Read the sentences in (2) and choose the correct response. Listen to his or her response (3). If it is correct, choose the next correct response to continue the conversation.

2. a. Sure. What would you like to know?
   b. Yes. I am more flexible than her.

4. a. He is single and has an older and a younger sister.
   b. My mother is very talkative, and my father is more optimistic.

6. a. How interesting! So, where was I? Oh, I also have eight siblings.
   b. No. Most of the couples in my family have only children.

8. I am the baby of the family.

Student B
What is the rule?

1. Look at the rules for student dorms. Ask Student A questions to fill in the blanks.

Example:

A: What is the rule about triple rooms?

B: All new students have triple rooms. What is the rule about fixing problems in the room?

A: All problems with the room must be reported to the dorm supervisor.

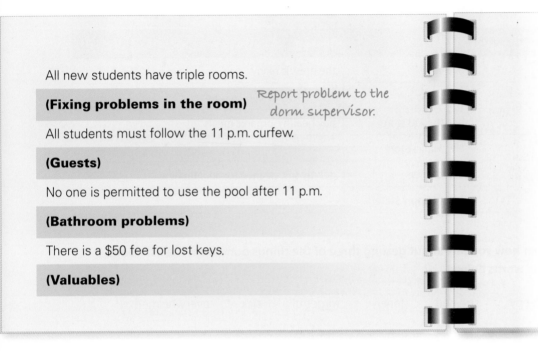

All new students have triple rooms.

(Fixing problems in the room) *Report problem to the dorm supervisor.*

All students must follow the 11 p.m. curfew.

(Guests)

No one is permitted to use the pool after 11 p.m.

(Bathroom problems)

There is a $50 fee for lost keys.

(Valuables)

Conversation Practice

2. Have a conversation with Student A (1–8). Listen to his or her sentence. Read the sentences in (2) and choose the correct response. Listen to his or her response (3). If it is correct, choose the next correct response to continue the conversation.

2. a. I'd be happy to help you. What is wrong?
   b. That's right. It may need a new light bulb.

4. a. I'll get someone to come to your room soon. Is that OK?
   b. Is one king-sized bed OK?

6. a. I can draw the route if you'd like.
   b. I only have a single room. Is that OK?

8. We'll send someone up right away.

pair with **Student A** ⓒ**CONFIDENCE BOOSTER** 5–8 *on p. 83*

Student B
What is the reason?

1a. Report the reasons for going to these places. Ask Student A questions to fill in the blanks.

Example:

A: Can you tell me why you have to go to the boutique?

B: The wedding planner said the dress was ready. Can you tell me why
   you need to go to the hair salon?

A: My hairstylist says my hair is too long.

Person	Place	Reason
wedding planner	boutique	the dress is ready
hairstylist	hair salon	my hair is too long
doctor	health food store	buy healthy, organic meals
	electronics store	
career counselor	dry cleaners	get my suit cleaned for an interview
	office supply store	

1b. Tell your partner how you feel about getting three of the things done from the list above.
Use three of the words below.

broke	sleepy	stressed	lonely	forgetful	sick	overwhelmed

Conversation Practice

2. Have a conversation with Student A (1–8). Listen to his or her sentence. Read the sentences in (2) and choose the correct response. Listen to his or her response (3). If it is correct, choose the next correct response to continue the conversation.

2. a. I'd be happy to help you. Can I ask why you want to join?
   b. I'm sorry, but I don't think that's a good idea.

4. a. I don't think walking up the stairs is a good idea.
   b. You'll love our gym! Can I please have your identification?

6. a. Certainly. This is a schedule of the pool hours. Here is your new membership card.
   b. Yes. What time are you free to make an appointment?

8. Really? I'm so sorry. Please accept my apology. I will make you a new card.

Student B
Nick used to play checkers.

1a. Look at the chart below. Ask and answer questions with *used to* and *used to be* to fill in the blanks.

Example:

A: Did Nick use to play checkers?

B: Yes, he did. Did Patty use to play hopscotch?

A: No, she didn't.

	Nick	Patty
play checkers	yes	
play hopscotch	no	*no*
go to the zoo	yes	
ride a bike around town	no	
donate toys to charity	no	
score goals in soccer	yes	
catch balls	yes	

1b. Tell Sudent A a story (you read, saw on TV, or heard from someone) that you think of when you see one of the words below. Respond to Student A's story with the words you think he or she is trying to talk about.

lucky	strange	awful	embarrassing	scary	disgusting	romantic

Example:

A: I remember when I was 12 years old, and it was the first day of school. When I got to my classroom, I tripped and fell down in front of the whole class.

B: How embarrassing!

Conversation Practice

2. Have a conversation with Student A (1–8). Listen to his or her sentence. Read the sentences in (2) and choose the correct response. Listen to his or her response (3). If it is correct, choose the next correct response to continue the conversation.

2. a. He released it on July 9, 2001. Why?

   b. It was earlier this year. Why do you ask?

4. a. Certainly. Your mother told me that she saw Michael Jordan in a restaurant.

   b. Oh, really? I wonder if they know each other.

6. a. How sad! They cancelled the program.

   b. How interesting! My brother works in the children's clinic, too!

8. I heard that, too.

Student B
How does she know him?

1a. Pam has many kinds of friends. Ask Student A questions about her friends to help you fill in the blanks.

Example:

A: How does Pam know Craig?

B: They were World History classmates. What kind of friend is Craig?

A: He's a fair-weather friend to Pam.

Name	How They Know Each Other	Type of Person	Type of Friend
Craig	World History class		*fair-weather friend*
Lily		reliable and caring	close friend
Yang	their moms are best friends		old friend
Cindy		loyal and supportive	

1b. Tell Student A about one of your friends. What is your friend's name? How did you meet? What type of friend and person is he or she?

Conversation Practice

2. Have a conversation with Student A (1–8). Listen to his or her sentence. Read the sentences in (2) and choose the correct response. Listen to his or her response (3). If it is correct, choose the next correct response to continue the conversation.

2. a. I wish I had remembered my friend's birthday. Did you?
   b. I have a lot of cyber friends from all over the world. Do you?

4. a. Really? I am very shy when I first meet someone in person. I feel much more comfortable online.
   b. Yes, she does, but they are just fair-weather friends. They aren't very close.

6. a. I'm really not sure. Maybe it's because I don't know what to talk about. I don't want to seem boring.
   b. I should have put a reminder about my friend's party in my phone.

8. That's a great idea. I can see myself joining the poetry club. Thanks for the advice!

Student B
What is the job?

1. Look at the job advertisement. Ask Student A questions to fill in the blanks.

Example:

A: What is the name of the language school?

B: Brighton English Language School. What kind of instructor are they looking for?

A: A full-time Italian instructor.

Brighton English Language School

Position:

_____ *full* - *time* _____ Italian Instructor

Education and Experience:

Preferred _____ degree with three years or more of work experience

Overseas work experience a plus

Responsibilities:

— teach _____ hours per week

— hold office hours four hours per week

— _____ advising

Requirements and Abilities:

— cover letter and resume

— three letters of _____ or three academic contacts with telephone and e-mail

— _____ in English

— excellent communication skills

— solid _____ skills

Conversation Practice

2. Have a conversation with Student A (1–8). Listen to his or her sentence. Read the sentences in (2) and choose the correct response. Listen to his or her response (3). If it is correct, choose the next correct response to continue the conversation.

2. a. Well, the main reason is that it's so easy to shop online.

   b. I certainly have. My grocery store now offers free babysitting while you shop.

4. a. I disagree. It looks like it could be an ad for shampoo.

   b. I agree. Also, a hardware store in town now gives free workshops on how to fix things.

6. Not yet. It's not in a convenient location for me.

How can we succeed?

1a. This is a brochure for new students. Ask Student A questions to fill in the blanks.

Example:

A: What is the most important skill for success?

B: Diligence. What is power?

A: Knowledge is power.

New Student Success

Diligence is the most important skill for success.

Follow the suggestions for success:

- _____ is power, so get as much as you can in your chosen field of study.

- Ignorance of the rules is no excuse for breaking them.

- Take a _____ of classes in your first two years because you may find you prefer another major.

- Keep all assignment deadlines in a _____.

- Expect to work hard.

Conversation Practice

2. Have a conversation with Student A (1–8). Listen to his or her sentence. Read the sentences in (2) and choose the correct response. Listen to his or her response (3). If it is correct, choose the next correct response to continue the conversation.

2. a. Yes, I do. To me it means laugh and you'll feel better. Do you have any idea what it means?
   b. I certainly do. Did you know that you should remove your shoes when you enter a Japanese house?

4. a. Oh, really? That's interesting. Do you know anything about American weddings?
   b. If you see a white cat at night, you'll have bad luck.

6. a. Yes, I do. It could mean you need to talk to everyone at the party to be polite.
   b. I heard you're not supposed to wear white because that's the bride's color.

8. Really? I didn't know that. Thanks for telling me.

What will you do?

1a. This is a list of things Angelica wants to do in the future. Ask Student A questions to fill in the blanks.

Example:

A: What will Angelica do with the things she doesn't use?

B: She will throw them out. What will she manage better?

A: She will manage her money better.

Angelica's Checklist for the Future

Immediate Future

☐ throw out the things I don't use

☐ manage my _____ better

☐ get in better shape by exercising regularly and losing _____

☐ buy a laptop

☐ go to _____ school in a major city

Distant Future

☐ get a good job

☐ get married

☐ have _____

1b. Put a check (✓) next to three items from Angelica's list that you want to do in your future. Tell Student A the reasons for your choices.

Conversation Practice

2. Have a conversation with Student A (1–8). Listen to his or her sentence. Read the sentences in (2) and choose the correct response. Listen to his or her response (3). If it is correct, choose the next correct response to continue the conversation.

2. a. That's bad for the environment because plastic breaks down slowly.

   b. I'm not completely sure, but I think I'd like to work for an environmental organization.

4. a. Well, I think a lot of changes could be made to cars. I'd like to create a cleaner fuel.

   b. Glass is definitely more expensive than plastic, but plastic breaks down slowly.

6. I disagree. We will find a cheaper fuel!

Audio and Video Scripts

LESSON 1
Conversation, Part C

John: Are you waiting for someone? Where are you going?

Isabel: Yeah, my brother. He's going to give me a ride home. We're having a party for my grandmother. It's her 80th birthday. Everyone will be there.

John: That's nice. Do you have a large family?

Isabel: I guess. Besides my mom and dad, I have three older brothers and two sisters.

John: Wow! You have a big family. I didn't know that.

Isabel: Do you have any siblings?

John: No, I'm an only child. It gets lonely sometimes.

Isabel: Really? Sometimes, I want to be alone!

LESSON 2
Listening, Part A and B

Maya: I volunteer three times a week after school. I go to an elementary school in an underdeveloped neighborhood and help students with their homework. They don't have private tutors and their parents are usually busy working. The kids look up to me and ask me for advice. I try to set a good example, and I encourage them to study hard.

Roberto: When I think about things, I try not to think too much about the negative side of things. I try to focus on the positive. I think things will work out for the best, and they usually do. Some of my friends are just the opposite, and that can be hard on me sometimes. I guess I prefer to be around people who also focus more on the positive. But I get that not everyone is the same.

Bernadette: I'm the type of person who tries to fix things. If I see something wrong, I try to make it right. It drives me crazy when I see a problem, and no one is doing anything about it. It's better to fix problems right away. I think this is a good quality to have. I just started a new job, and my boss seems really pleased with my work so far. Some people just accept a problem. But it doesn't have to be that way. It always feels satisfying when I can solve something.

Young-ho: My sister is a real people person, but I'm just the opposite. I prefer to do things on my own more. I like people, of course, but I also really enjoy my own time. I read a lot, go for walks by myself, things like that. I have friends and we have a lot of fun together, but I guess I prefer being on my own. Some people think that's a bad thing, but I don't think so.

LESSON 3
Conversation, Part C

Sara: It must be fun having a sister about the same age as you.

Keisha: Well, sometimes it is.

Sara: How similar are you and Kelly? Or are you really different?

Keisha: Well, we're both pretty reliable. But I think I'm more reliable than Kelly.

Sara: Well, you are two years older. How are you different?

Keisha: She's more flexible than me. She's *a lot* more flexible.

Sara: What do you mean?

Keisha: She's the type of person who just goes with things. And Kelly is also really forgiving. She lives by the motto, "*Forgive and forget.*" I forgive, but I never forget.

LESSON 4

Listening, Part A and B

Rachel: Did you read that story about the woman who works two jobs to help pay for her kids' education?

Peter: No.

Rachel: She's amazing. She works as a school nurse during the day, and then at night she works at a hospital. She works about 70 hours a week. She—

Lena: Sorry to interrupt, Rachel, but why was the story important to you?

Rachel: Well, I admire that she was sacrificing her own happiness for her kids. That's a value that's important to me. She thinks of others before she thinks of herself. What do you think?

Lena: I guess I don't see it the same way. I think she doesn't spend a lot of time with her kids, and that isn't always good.

Rachel: That's a good point, but her kids are in college.

Peter: You seem to feel strongly about this. What other values do you find important?

Rachel: Oh, there are several. I really look up to and respect my parents. And I hope that others respect me.

Lena: What else?

Rachel: Being sympathetic is also important. I think we all have to try to help each other.

Peter: I think sportsmanship is important. And friendship. What do you think, Rachel?

Rachel: To me kindness is more important than friendship and sportsmanship. It's—

Peter: Can I ask a question? How can friendship not be important?

Rachel: I'm not saying it isn't. But what I value is kindness. I expect that from my friends, and hope other people are kind to me. Do you see what I mean?

Peter: I do. I feel the same way.

LESSONS 1–4 ENGLISH IN ACTION

Maria: This is perfect. We get to go to New York City! I'm so excited!

Eric: Is the hotel you and Jill staying in OK?

Maria: I think so. It looked really nice in the pictures. Are you nervous about staying with Eric's family?

Tom: Not at all! I'm excited to meet them. Especially his brother. Where is Jill, by the way?

Maria: I don't know. She said she was on her way.

Eric: She always says that. Well, we still have some time left before our bus.

Maria: So, Eric. What's your brother like?

Eric: He's the first-born. He's a people person, so he has lots of friends. And he has an awesome job. He makes apps for smartphones. He's an innovator and a problem solver.

Maria: Wow. He sounds so cool.

Tom: Yeah…I can't wait to meet him. He's my role model.

Eric: Sometimes, I wish I were more like him. He's more sociable than me, too.

Tom: Hey! So are you! And you're really…

Maria: Considerate!

Eric: Thanks guys.

Maria: Sorry to interrupt, but I just got a text from Jill that she's on her way down.

Eric: So, what was I talking about?

Tom: Your brother and how he's sociable.

Eric: Right.

Tom: I think we can learn a lot of values from our family members.

Jill: Sorry guys.

Eric: Jill, we're only going to be there for two days.

Jill: I know. Wait.

Tom: What?

Jill: I forgot something upstairs.

Eric: What did you forget?

Jill: I definitely need another shirt.

Eric/Maria/: NO!
Tom

LESSON 5
Conversation, Part C

Mira: Hello. I'd like to check in, please. My name's Mira Abboud. I have a reservation.

Hotel clerk: Yes, I have your reservation here, Ms. Abboud. May I have your passport?

Mira: Here you are. By the way, is there wireless Internet in the room?

Hotel clerk: Yes, but for a fee. It's free in the lobby. Can I have your credit card, please?

Mira: Sure. Here is my card.

Hotel clerk: Thank you. Let me confirm this for you. You have a single room for four nights, checking out on the 16th. Is there anything more I can do for you?

Mira: I don't think so. Thank you. You've been very helpful.

Hotel clerk: You're welcome. Enjoy your stay.

LESSON 6
Listening, Part A and B

Sandra: Excuse me. Are you the building manager?

Manager: Yes. My name's Jimmy. Jimmy Coburn.

Sandra: I'm Sandra Smith. I just moved into apartment 4C. I got these building rules, and I just have a few questions. Do you have a minute?

Manager: Sure.

Sandra: It won't take long. The first question I have is about parking.

Manager: Right. You can park anywhere. There are no assigned parking spots.

Sandra: I was confused because there was no parking sign in front of the building.

Manager: Oh, that. You need to keep the area in front of the building clear. In case of emergencies. There are plenty of spaces in the back.

Sandra: OK. And are there rules about parties?

Manager: No one is allowed to have parties on weekdays. We want things quiet for everyone here. You can have parties on weekends. But you have to finish any party before midnight.

Sandra: I see. That's good. I'm not much of a partier. And what is this here, about no keys for visitors?

Manager: Oh, you're permitted to have guests, of course, but we can't give anyone a key. They would have to borrow yours, if they needed one.

Sandra: All right.

Manager: Anything else?

Sandra: Yes, the last one, I promise, is about cats. You see I have—

Manager: That's fine.

Sandra: So, we're allowed to have cats?

Manager: Yes, just not dogs.

Sandra: Not even small dogs?

Manager: No dogs, period. Is that OK?

Sandra: That's great, actually. My cats hate dogs.

Manager: *Cats?*

Sandra: Yes, my cats. There's Mitzi, Snowball, Charlie, Little Miss Perfect, Trouble, Sweet Pea, and Penelope.

LESSON 7
Conversation, Part C

Hotel clerk: Front desk. How can I help you?

Guest: Hi, I just checked in. There are some problems with my room. I'm in room 429.

Hotel clerk: Oh, sorry to hear that. What are the problems?

Guest: Well, first the bedside lamp isn't working at all.

Hotel clerk: It may need a new light bulb.

Guest: That's what I thought. And the faucet in the bathroom is leaking. I can't turn it off.

Hotel clerk: OK. I'll get someone to come and look at it right away.

Guest: Thank you. And one more thing. There are no towels in the bathroom.

Hotel clerk: I'll ask housekeeping to send you some now.

Guest: Great. I really appreciate it. Thanks very much.

Hotel clerk: Thank you for your patience.

LESSON 8
Listening, Part A and B

1. A: Excuse me. What time do we land?

   B: At 10:45. We have another hour or so.

   A: OK, thank you.

   B: Is Denver your final destination?

   A: No, I'm transferring to Los Angeles. I just hope I can make it.

   B: I can check on your connecting flight.

   A: Oh, that would be great. Thank you so much.

2. A: Hi.

   B: Can I help you?

   A: I'd like my car, please.

   B: Would you like me to get your car now?

   A: Yes, thank you.

   B: Um, I have your key, but I need the card with the number I gave you earlier.

   A: Oh, I'm sorry, of course. Here it is.

   B: I'll just be a minute.

3. A: And here is your change.

   B: Thank you.

   A: Is it a gift?

   B: Yes, it's for my parents. It's their anniversary.

   A: I'm sure they'll love it. I can wrap it for you if you'd like.

   B: You can?

   A: Certainly.

   B: That would be great.

4. A: How was everything?

   B: It was excellent, thank you.

   A: Do you want me to bring you a dessert menu?

   B: Oh, I don't know.

   A: We're famous for our desserts.

   B: Oh, why not? It never hurts to just look.

5. A: Guest services.
   B: Yes, I'm in room 70—I just checked in.
   A: Yes?
   B: And there's a party in the room across the hall. It's pretty noisy.
   A: Would you like me to change your room?
   B: Oh, could you?
   A: Of course. Let me just see what I have available. Please hold.

LESSONS 5–8 ENGLISH IN ACTION

Maria: Wow, this hotel is really nice.
Jill: Yeah. It's better than the pictures. Good afternoon. We are here to check in.
Hotel clerk: Hello. Do you have a reservation?
Maria: Yes, we do.
Hotel clerk: Can I have the name of the person who made the reservation?
Jill: Jill Willcox. W-I-L-L-C-O-X.
Hotel clerk: Thank you. Hm… looks like there is no reservation.
Jill: But, I'm sure I made a reservation.
Hotel clerk: I have a Till Millfox.
Jill: That's me. Just spelled wrong.
Hotel clerk: May I see your driver's license? But it says Jill Willcox. And the reservation is for Till Millfox.
Jill: Right. The person must have took down the wrong name.
Hotel clerk: I see.
Maria: Can we speak to the manager?
Hotel clerk: I'll call him. Bob? This is Pam from the front desk. I have a Jill Willcox who says the reservation was made as Till Millfox. Uh huh. Hm…huh. OK. Thanks.
Jill: What did he say?
Hotel clerk: Nothing. It was his voicemail.
Maria: Listen. We paid for the hotel.
Jill: Here's the credit card.

Hotel clerk: Very well. So, you are Till!
Jill: No. Yes. Nevermind.
Hotel clerk: Here are your room keys. You can help yourself to hot tea and coffee in your room. You can't make noise after midnight and you can't have any parties.
Maria: OK. No parties.
Jill: Thank you.

[A few moments later…]
Hotel clerk: Front desk. Who? Till?
Jill: No, it's Jill—yes. It's Till Millfox from room 401.
Hotel clerk: Oh, hi. How can I help you?
Jill: The light in our room isn't working.
Hotel clerk: Oh. Would you like me to send someone to fix it?
Jill: Yes.
Hotel clerk: I'd be happy to call Bob for you.
Jill: OK. Will he come soon?
Hotel clerk: As soon as he answers the phone.
Jill: OK, thank you.
Maria: Jill?
Jill: I'm on the phone.
Maria: I can't see anything!
Jill: Please, send someone soon.
Hotel clerk: I can bring some flashlights while you wait.
Jill: Yes. Thank you!
Hotel clerk: Now where are those flashlights? Here they are.

LESSON 9
Conversation, Part C

Mark: So, what's it like living here? It looks like a convenient place to live.
Anne: Oh, it is. The only thing is there's a lot of construction. But I really like it, and everything I need is close by. And my neighbors are friendly.

Mark: Sounds great! Actually, I need to do a few things this weekend. Do you know where I can get a haircut?

Anne: I'd go to Paul's Hair Salon just down the street. It's really popular.

Mark: And do you know if it's expensive?

Anne: I don't think so. A haircut is $20 or so. That's reasonable.

Mark: That's not too bad. Where is it?

Anne: It's next to Super Foods. You can take a bus there. There's one every 20 minutes.

LESSON 10
Listening, Part A and B

1. Frank: And here you are. If you could just sign that for me…

    Customer 1: Um…

    Frank: Is everything OK?

    Customer 1: I'm afraid this isn't mine.

    Frank: What?

    Customer 1: This is not what I ordered. And this is not my card.

    Frank: I'm so sorry. Then, someone else has yours.

    Customer 1: That's not good.

    Frank: I'll bring you the correct one. Just a moment, please. Please excuse me. It's my first day.

2. Frank: And here we are.

    Customer 2: What's this?

    Frank: It's your steak.

    Customer 2: My steak? What steak?

    Frank: You didn't order a steak?

    Customer 2: No. I'm a vegetarian.

    Frank: Let me just check this…oh, I see. This goes to table five. My apologies. I'll go get your order.

    Customer 2: Thank you.

    Frank: And I'll bring you a free dessert later.

    Customer 2: Oh, that's not necessary.

3. Customer 2: Excuse me.

    Frank: Yes?

    Customer 2: I don't think this is correct. You gave me too much change.

    Frank: Are you sure?

    Customer 2: Yes, my total was $17.50. I paid with a twenty. My change should be two-fifty.

    Frank: And what did I give you?

    Customer 2: Three-fifty. See?

    Frank: Oh, yes. Please just keep it.

    Customer 2: No, no.

    Frank: It's fine really.

4. Customer 3: Check, please.

    Frank: Yours…is…right here.

    Customer 3: Thank you. Oh, just a second, please. This doesn't seem right.

    Frank: Why am I not surprised? Nothing is going right today.

    Customer 3: It's correct except for this. Look here. You charged me for two desserts.

    Frank: Ah, yes. I don't know how that happened. Please accept my apologies. I'll bring you a new bill.

    Customer 3: OK.

    Frank: It'll be just a minute.

    Customer 3: Can I have some more coffee while I wait?

LESSON 11

Conversation, Part C

Receptionist: Good morning. Dr. Kim's office. How can I help you?

Heather: Hello. I'd like to make an appointment to see Dr. Kim.

Receptionist: What is your name, please?

Heather: Heather Jenson.

Receptionist: I can get you an appointment this Thursday. Can you come in at 11:15?

Heather: Um…I'd prefer something in the afternoon. I work in the morning.

Receptionist: Would you be able to come in on Friday at 3:30? Are you free then?

Heather: Let me see…yes, that's fine.

Receptionist: OK. So your appointment is with Dr. Kim at 3:30 on Friday the 20th. Please come about 15 minutes early.

Heather: Great! Thank you!

LESSON 12

Listening, Part A

Lindsay: Why do I never seem to have any money? I have a part-time job, but I'm always broke. I have so many bills, and I feel like I'm always spending on clothes, food, and entertainment.

Dylan: You probably just don't realize how you spend money. I'm sure if you just made some changes you'd feel like you had enough spending money.

Lindsay: What kind of changes? What could I do?

Dylan: One thing you could do is stop taking taxis. I notice you often take taxis.

Lindsay: That's a good idea.

Dylan: Just try to walk when possible.

Lindsay: I like that idea, too. It'll save money and exercise is always good.

Dylan: And something else you could do is drink less coffee and soda.

Lindsay: Hm…I don't really like that idea. I need my caffeine in the afternoon.

Dylan: OK, but the money you spend on drinks really adds up to a lot. Anyway, another thing you could do is cancel your magazine subscriptions.

Lindsay: I'll do it. I should read more books anyway.

Dylan: And do you shop a lot?

Lindsay: I guess. Hey, do you like my new jacket?

Dylan: Um, sure. You could buy only clothes that are on sale.

Lindsay: You're funny. No. I don't like that idea.

Dylan: OK…well, another idea is to keep a weekly budget.

Lindsay: Every week?

Dylan: And if I could make one recommendation, it would be this—cut up your credit cards.

Lindsay: Are you crazy? I hate that idea. I *really* hate that idea.

Dylan: Just trying to help.

Lindsay: Oh, I know. And I appreciate it. Say, let me take you to lunch. It will be my treat.

LESSONS 9–12 ENGLISH IN ACTION

Maria: We have some time before we meet Eric and Tom.

Jill: We should walk around and go shopping!

Maria: I want to do my hair, too!

Jill: That sounds fun! Where should we begin?

Maria: Let's ask the hotel clerk. I'm sure she can recommend places to visit.

Jill: Hi, Pam.

Pam: Good morning.

Maria: We want to look around. Can you tell us where we should go?

Pam: Sure! I have pictures I can show you, too. One thing you should do is walk around Central Park. It's in the heart of the city. You can get a cool view of the city.

Jill: That's a great idea. Do you know any good places to eat?

Pam: The East Village is great. You can get Indian food, Japanese food, just about everything!

Maria: Can you tell us if it's expensive?

Pam: It's cheap compared to the rest of the city. Oh, and another thing you should do is go to Times Square! It's beautiful at night.

Jill: What about shopping?

Pam: Oh, go to Soho. It can be crowded, but there are tons of shops in that area.

Maria: Wow. Is there also a place where I can get a cool hairstyle?

Pam: Hm…I know a guy who does fabulous hairstyles. Here's his business card.

Jill: I'm afraid you gave me a room key.

Pam: Oh! Sorry.

Jill: That's OK.

Pam: Here it is. Have fun, ladies!

[Later that day…]

Tom: They should be here soon.

Eric: Wait. I think that's them.

Jill: Hi, guys! I had such a great time today!

Tom: Hi, Jill. Where's Maria?

Jill: She should be here soon. I think that's her…

Tom: That's definitely not Maria. Um…nice. Um…day huh?

Jill: Yeah.

Maria: Did you guys notice?

Eric: Hm…notice what?

Maria: My hair. It's the coolest hair style I've ever had! So New York!

Jill: It's definitely fabulous.

Maria: You guys should totally go to Daniel LaBute's salon, too!

Jill: Oh, and we're late! Let's go!

LESSON 13
Conversation, Part C

Zoe: What kind of childhood did you have, Max? Were you happy?

Max: I had a great childhood.

Zoe: What do you remember about it?

Max: Lots of things. For example, my parents had a karaoke machine. My friends and I would pretend we were on TV. I was always the star!

Zoe: How fun!

Max: What sort of things did you do as a kid?

Zoe: Oh, I was a tomboy! I used to play baseball. Sometimes, I miss it.

LESSON 14
Listening, Part A and B

Chelsea: Hello.

Inez: Chelsea? It's Inez. Guess what!

Chelsea: Um…what?

Inez: I won a contest. I entered an online contest, and I won! The prize is a trip to Paris!

Chelsea: No way. Are you serious?

Inez: I'm serious. I can't believe it.

Chelsea: How lucky!

Inez: The thing is…I don't remember entering an online contest.

Chelsea: That's strange. Are you sure the contest is real?

Inez: It is. They called me, and I already have the tickets.

Chelsea: How long is the trip for?

Inez: It will be for one week.

Chelsea: Well, congratulations, Inez. I'm really happy for you.

Inez: Listen, Chelsea, what are you doing in January? I want you to go with me.

Chelsea: Really?

Inez: Yes!

Chelsea: Inez, you're the best! Thanks!

LESSON 15

Conversation, Part C

Aaron: I saw an interesting new story about a 10-year-old boy who wrote a children's book. His name is Cameron Titus and the book is called *Cameron's A–Z*.

Molly: Really? That's fantastic.

Aaron: The towns near him had some bad storms. He wanted to help, so he donated all the money he made to the charity, Habitat for Humanity. They build homes.

Molly: What a great kid. And generous, too!

Aaron: He's already started to write a second book, too. He's donating all that money as well—to a local hospital.

LESSON 16

Listening, Part A and B

Host: And welcome back to *As Luck Would Have It*. If you're just joining us, we're here with Walter. Walter is only five questions away from a million dollars. Walter, you can walk away at any time, if you don't like the question. Answer all six, and you receive one million dollars. Ready to keep playing?

Walter: Yes, let's hear the next question.

Host: All right. When did the Titanic sink? I just need the year.

Walter: April 15, 1912.

Host: And you are correct! I'll read the next question. Who hosted the Olympics in 1988?

Walter: Let's see. It's either Spain or South Korea. I think Spain was after Korea. I remember the Olympics were in Barcelona in 1992. Yes, that's right. So my answer is South Korea.

Host: You're not sounding so confident, Walter.

Walter: No, I'm sure. South Korea.

Host: Yes! For this next question I will need a date—a month, a day, and a year. OK? When did man first land on the moon?

Walter: I know it was in July 1969. You need a day, huh?

Host: I'm afraid so. Let me remind you that you have right now $250,000. If you answer this you will have half a million dollars.

Walter: I'm pretty sure I know this. I remember I got up and watched it with my parents because it was an important day in history.

Host: Take your time.

Walter: It was the 20th. That's it! July 20, 1969. Yes?

Host: Yes! Congratulations, Walter. We're almost out of time. Let's go to our final question. Ready? In what decade did the first 3D movie come out? 3D movies are very popular today, but when was the first one? Audience, no help please!

Walter: I remember seeing lots of black and white photos of people in the 1950s with glasses on, watching movies. I'm pretty sure it was the 1950s.

Host: This is for a million dollars...if you are wrong—you go home with nothing.

Walter: I'm going for it! I'm going to say the 1950s.

Host: The answer is...the 1920s! Oh, Walter, I'm so sorry. The first 3D movie was in 1922 and it was called *The Power of Love*. I hope you've enjoyed being a contestant on *As Luck Would Have It*, Walter. Walter? Walter?

LESSONS 13–16 ENGLISH IN ACTION

Tom: Whoo. It feels good to be back home.

Eric: Definitely. Tom? Did you close the window before we left?

Tom: Of course, I did.

Eric: But the window is open. Things all over the floor.

Tom: Strange! Maybe it was the wind.

Eric: I think we've been robbed. I'm missing something.

Tom: Oh, no! Let me check my room. Everything is in my room. And the TV is here. What are you missing?

Eric: I don't understand. Why would anyone take Brownie?

Tom: Eric, I'm sorry, but what Brownie? Was it really valuable?

Eric: Well, my grandmother gave it to me when I was a kid. It must be worth a lot of money right now! It's an antique!

Tom: I read an interesting story online about a person sold an old object from the eighteen-hundreds thinking it wasn't worth anything—turned out to be an antique worth over a million dollars.

Eric: Wow, Tom. Thanks.

Tom: I'm sorry, probably not the best time to tell you that.

Eric: We should call the police.

Tom: Um…

Eric: Can you do it? I'm very upset right now. Please?! Please?!

Tom: OK…hi, is this the local police station?

Eric: Tell them we've been robbed and I'm very upset.

Tom: Eric, my roommate, believes we have been robbed.

Eric: Tell them I'm very upset.

Tom: He says he is really upset. Mm…hm. No, the TV is here. Actually everything is here.

Eric: Except my antique. My grandmother gave it to me in 1996!

Tom: Right. He's telling me he's missing an antique from 1996. Mm hm…Hold on. What does it look like?

Eric: It's round. It's very small. It's brown.

Tom: What is it exactly?

Eric: I have a picture of it. Here.

Tom: It's uh…it's a teddy bear. Right. OK, thank you officer.

Eric: What did they say?

Tom: That a teddy bear from 1996 is not an antique.

Eric: Well, this is just awful! What could've happened?

Tom: Eric? Is this Brownie?

Eric: Yes!

Tom: It was underneath the sofa.

Eric: How did it get there? Tom? Tom?

LESSON 17

Conversation, Part C

Kal: Hi, it's Kal. Do you have a minute? It's about my best friend Brad. You know him, right?

Winnie: Sure. Is everything OK?

Kal: Yeah. I just feel like we're acquaintances these days.

Winnie: You do? Why?

Kal: He doesn't really call or text me much anymore. His mind seems to be somewhere else, too. The other day—

Winnie: Sorry, but can I interrupt for a second?

Kal: Of course. Go ahead.

Winnie: I think Brad got a part-time job.

Kal: He did? I had no idea.

Winnie: Yeah. I saw him at the coffee shop the other day, but he was working there!

Kal: Oh, I should really be a better friend!

LESSON 18

Listening, Part A and B

1. I have this friend named Jonathan. He's been a close friend for a long time. Last month, I asked to borrow some money from him. It wasn't a lot, and I said I'd pay him back in a week. A week went by, and I didn't have the money, so I said I'd pay the following week. He got all upset with me and said he needed the money right away. I mean, it's only another week, so I don't know what the big deal is. I managed to get the money together, and I just paid him. He didn't say thank you or anything, and I'm now afraid I may have lost his friendship over this.

2. My friend Casey is probably my best friend. She's honest, reliable, and truthful—all qualities that are important for me in a friendship. Well, the other day I was telling her about my sister. My sister was mad at me because I didn't remember her birthday. I told my sister she was acting silly and now she is hardly talking to me. Well, I was telling this to Casey, and she thought I was wrong. She really made me see that I was being insensitive and, my behavior wasn't very nice. That's what I like about Casey—she can help me see things that I wouldn't normally see.

3. I have a lot of friends, or at least I thought I did. But I now see some of these friends more as acquaintances. Let me explain. Last month, I was in a car accident. It wasn't very serious, but I did have to spend some time in the hospital. It was hard because I missed classes and was behind on my homework. The strange thing is, only three of my friends came to visit me. And no one else called or sent cards—nothing. It kind of hurt my feelings. What is interesting is that it's helped me realize who my true friends are. I thought I had more close friends, but I see now that's not the case. That's fine with me, actually. What's important to me is to have a few really close, good friends.

4. I really miss my old friend Patrick. He's always been there for me—really supportive and a good listener, but I can't say we're really friends anymore, and it makes me sad. We just started to grow apart. We call each other less often and don't see each other much either, maybe once a month. I think it's my fault. Maybe I didn't work at our friendship enough and just assumed we'd always be friends. But I think you do need to work on your friendships. Otherwise people grow apart. I don't know what to do about it. I could accept things like they are or possibly reach out to Patrick and try to make more time for him.

LESSON 19

Listening, Part A and B

1. **Abigail:** I'd like to make some new friends. What would you suggest?

   John: You want new friends?

   Abigail: Well, I want more friends. I like my friends now.

   John: Oh, good. Well, I think you should join a class. That's what I did. I took a language class. I always wanted to learn Spanish, so I took a class twice a week. I really wanted a small class, and one that focused on conversation. It worked. I learned some Spanish and made some great new friends.

   Abigail: That sounds like it could be fun.

   John: It is.

2. **Sarah:** So, I hear you're looking for ways to make more friends. John told me.

   Abigail: Yeah. He suggested I take a class.

   Sarah: I have a better idea. You should just introduce yourself to people. Not strangers, but people at school, at parties, in the cafeteria, places like that.

   Abigail: Do you do that? Just introduce yourself to people?

   Sarah: Sure!

   Abigail: I wouldn't feel comfortable doing that. That feels a little too forward for me personally. But thanks for the suggestion.

3. **Abigail:** Can I ask you something?

   Eliza: Sure.

   Abigail: I'm trying to enlarge my circle of friends, you know, to have more friends. What do you think is the best way to do that?

   Eliza: Well, have you thought about doing volunteer work?

   Abigail: Volunteer work? You mean work for free?

   Eliza: Of course. Volunteering is a great thing to do. You meet a lot of people that way. And you're doing something good.

   Abigail: I might find that interesting. I'll look into it.

   Eliza: You know, that's how I met a lot of my friends.

4. **Abigail:** What do you think is the best way to make friends?

   Brandon: If you want to make friends, you should play sports.

   Abigail: Play sports?

   Brandon: Yeah. Play a team sport.

   Abigail: That doesn't really appeal to me.

   Brandon: Why not?

   Abigail: I don't know—I'm just not that into sports. But I appreciate the idea.

   Brandon: No problem.

5. **Abigail:** You have a lot of friends, Gary. How do you do it?

   Gary: Make friends?

   Abigail: Yeah. I know you go to parties. Would you suggest that?

   Gary: No. Actually, I'd join a student club.

   Abigail: What kind of student club?

   Gary: It doesn't matter. Whatever interests you.

   Abigail: Hm…I can see myself doing that. Thanks.

LESSON 20
Conversation, Part C

Brett: You'll never guess what happened. My friend John invited me to a party at his house last night, and I totally forgot about it. I feel awful.

Dana: Oh, no. How come?

Brett: I was so busy all week that it completely slipped my mind. I wish I'd remembered because it was his birthday.

Dana: Have you talked to him? Was he upset?

Brett: Not yet. I don't know what to do. What do you think?

Dana: What you could do is call John now and apologize. I always say honesty is the best policy.

Brett: That's a good idea.

LESSONS 17–20 ENGLISH IN ACTION
[Coffee Shop]

Maria: Tom isn't picking up my phone calls.

Jill: He isn't answering mine either.

Eric: He must be really upset.

Maria: I can't believe we forgot his birthday.

Eric: I feel the worst! I live with him and I forgot.

Jill: One thing you can do is talk to him when he gets home.

Eric: He's not really talking to me.

Maria: We should have remembered.

Jill: He's not just an acquaintance either. He always says birthdays are his favorite days.

Maria: What if we tell him that we remembered! We just didn't say anything.

Jill: I think I could do that.

Eric: I wouldn't feel comfortable doing that. We should be honest.

Jill: What we should do is find him and apologize.

Eric: I agree.

Jill: Oh! I have an idea.

Maria: What?

Jill: What's Tom's favorite thing?

Eric: Pasta?

Jill: OK…second favorite thing.

Maria and Eric: Oh yeah…great idea!

Jill: Check please?

[Later that day…]

Tom: Happy birthday yesterday to me. Happy birthday dear Tom even though it was yesterday. Happy birthday yesterday to me.

Tom: Hello? Anyone there?

Eric, Jill, Maria: SURPRISE!

Jill: Tom! It's just us!

Eric: Tom, we're sorry we forgot.

Jill: We're really sorry.

Tom: Guys…it's OK! This is the best birthday ever! It's two of my favorite things, pasta and surprises!

LESSON 21
Listening, Part A and B

Interviewer: So, let's continue our interview. Why are you interested in this job?

Doug: I'm a people person.

Interviewer: Are you OK working the night shift?

Doug: Actually, no. I have class in the morning, so I can only work in the afternoon.

Interviewer: That's OK. We have several positions available.

Doug: Oh, good. I can work any afternoon except Wednesdays.

Interviewer: What are some things you are good at?

Doug: I'm good with computers. And I'm also good with languages. I speak Spanish and a little Japanese.

Interviewer: What are your salary expectations?

Doug: I'd prefer not to say, if that's OK. I'm sure I'll be fine with the standard salary.

Interviewer: Um…OK.

Doug: I assume we can talk about salary later?

Interviewer: Oh, of course. Let's go onto our next question. How would someone describe you?

Doug: Wow, that's a tough question.

Interviewer: Take your time.

Doug: People say I have a lot of confidence. And that I'm very organized.

Interviewer: Well, that's good. And what is your greatest weakness?

Doug: My greatest weakness? I think that I work too hard.

Interviewer: You work too hard?

Doug: Yes, sometimes I don't take enough time for me.

Interviewer: I understand.

Doug: Can I ask a question?

Interviewer: Of course.

Doug: I was wondering if…

LESSON 22
Conversation, Part C

John: What do you think this ad could be for?

Amanda: I'm not sure. It looks like it could be for shampoo. Doesn't it?

John: Shampoo? Maybe. I think it's probably for hair coloring. I'm not sure.

Amanda: That's possible. Or I wonder if it's advertising cosmetics. It's hard to tell.

John: Whatever it is, I don't think it's very effective. It needs to be more clear. What do you think makes a good advertisement?

Amanda: Ads don't need to say much to be effective. They need to be simple and direct.

LESSON 23
Conversation, Part C

Jan: How's the store doing Phil? It looks different.

Phil: Well, I've made some changes. People are buying fewer and fewer books from book stores these days.

Jan: But why is that? Are people reading less?

Phil: The main reason is that it's so easy to shop online and buy e-books.

Jan: So, what changes have you made?

Phil: We are bringing in authors for book signings.

Jan: That's a great idea!

Phil: People like to meet authors and hear them read.

Jan: That's true. People can't do that online.

Phil: Yes. And we've just opened this coffee shop. Let's get a cup!

LESSON 24
Listening, Part A

Host: Hello, and thanks for joining me on this week's show. I'm your host Gillian Chisholm and here with me today is Adam Brown, author of the new book, *Running a Small Business*. Welcome to the show, Adam.

Adam: Thanks for having me.

Gillian: So, what's important in running a small business?

Adam: Every business is different. What is necessary to run a restaurant will be different from what is needed to run an Internet café or an electronics store. For example, some people say that location is everything. We hear, "Location, location, location." That may be important for a restaurant or a hair salon, but not for all businesses. Word of mouth can make a restaurant in an inconvenient location a success. And the best location in the world won't help a poorly run business, no matter what.

Gillian: So is there anything that you can say is true for all businesses?

Adam: Yes, all businesses need to have great customer service and quality products.

Listening, Part B

Adam: I have three things that I talk about in the first chapter of my book. The most important thing to remember is that for any business you need to make as much money as you can from what you sell or the service you provide. That may seem obvious but you'd be surprised how often people don't do this. One way to do it is to up-sell.

Gillian: Up-sell?

Adam: To up-sell is to sell other things in addition to your main product. For example, coffee shops sell tea, juice, cookies, and more. They up-sell other products besides coffee.

Gillian: That's great advice.

Adam: The second thing is to keep costs down. Low costs help increase the money you make. You might find cheaper ways to do things, do some things yourself—there are many, many things you can do—use your imagination. The third thing is to pay your employees well.

Gillian: Pay your employees well? But that's adding costs.

Adam: I thought you might say that. If you pay your employees less, you might make more money in the short term, but believe me, employees won't work for you long.

Gillian: I hope *my* boss is listening. Do you hear that?

Adam: It's really—

Gillian: Sorry, but I have to interrupt for one minute, as I need to go to a commercial break. I'll be back with Adam Brown after this short break.

LESSONS 21–24 ENGLISH IN ACTION

Interviewer: Sorry to keep you waiting.

Tom: Oh, it was no wait at all.

Interviewer: It looks like you received excellent grades at university. You have the computer skills we need.

Tom: Great.

Interviewer: But then there are many students with excellent grades and computer skills. What makes you different?

Tom: Uh. Well. Uh. People say that I'm a um…confident. A hard worker.

Interviewer: People say…or you know?

Tom: I know. I'm confident, a hard worker, *and* I'm reliable and trustworthy.

Interviewer: How are you reliable and trustworthy?

Tom: When I'm given a task or responsibility, I make sure I do my best. I don't let other people down.

Interviewer: OK. What is your greatest weakness?

Tom: Some people say…no…I know my greatest weakness is that I'm sometimes too focused.

Interviewer: That's not always a bad thing is it?

Tom: No.

Interviewer: Why do you want to work in advertising?

Tom: It's creative, interesting, and I know I can do a great job.

Interviewer: OK. Let's see how great you are. I want to use this picture in an ad. What do you think it's for?

Tom: The environment?

Interviewer: Come on. You said creative.

Tom: Hm…I would use this image for a paper company that uses recyclable paper. I would use the words, "We save trees."

Interviewer: That's a cool idea. It's definitely more creative than your first answer. What do you think is needed for an ad to be successful?

Tom: I think a good ad needs to be original.

Interviewer: OK. Fewer and fewer people are buying books from bookstores nowadays. What is the reason?

Tom: The main reasons are that online access is more convenient and people have less time in their schedules.

Interviewer: Everyone knows those reasons. What else?

Tom: Online stores have better ads?

Interviewer: Online stores have ads *everywhere*. That is the difference. OK, this went well. Nice job. We'll let you know in a few days. Thanks, Tom.

Tom: Thank you!

LESSON 25
Conversation, Part C

Dan: So, what are some of the things I need to know when I'm in China?

Sarah: OK. Well, you're supposed to take off your shoes before you enter someone's home.

Dan: OK. That's the same in Japan and Korea.

Sarah: That's right. And when you visit someone's home, it's the custom to bring a small gift. Just don't give a clock.

Dan: OK. That's good to know.

Sarah: But in China, if someone gives you a gift, you're not supposed to open it right away. That would be very impolite.

Dan: Got it! Thanks for the tips!

LESSON 26
Listening, Part B

1. I was watching TV last night—one of those talent shows. There was this one guy that got up to sing. He looked kind of strange. He wasn't very good-looking and he wasn't dressed very well. I wasn't expecting much, to be honest. But then he opened his mouth and started to sing. The audience went crazy. He was incredible. I wasn't expecting him to be so talented.

2. I have this nephew. His name is Johnny, and he's a pretty good kid. I try to act as a role model for him, you know, to teach him right from wrong. I give him advice and tell him how to behave. But he doesn't always do what I tell him. He sometimes acts just like me, even if it's not the best way to act. It's frustrating—I wish he'd listen to me more and not just copy what I do.

3. I saw this Italian motorcycle that looked really cool. I decided right then and there to buy it. I couldn't really afford it, but I bought it anyway. Well, it's been giving me headaches ever since. I don't have a place to park it, so I have to pay for a parking spot. And I didn't know, but it uses a lot of gas. Gas is really expensive these days. It seemed like a good idea at the time, but I know now I should have thought about it before buying it.

4. I just got my exam results this morning, and I did really poorly. I wanted to study last night for my exam, but my friend called me and invited me to a movie. I went and then we went out for pizza. I got home really late, so I didn't study at all. And of course I didn't do well. I'm so stupid! Why didn't I stay home and study last night?

5. Last month, I won some money in a contest. I just entered and won! How lucky is that? Anyway, after I got the prize money I went a little crazy. I took a short vacation with my friend Wendy. I took her to Hawaii with me. I bought some nice clothes, ate at a few expensive restaurants, and before I knew it, I spent all my prize money. It's like it just disappeared! My life doesn't feel that different, almost like it never happened.

LESSON 27

Listening, Part A and B

Mark: It's great that we finally set the date for our wedding. I'm sure the weather in June will be nice.

Lesley: Now the real fun can start—the wedding planning.

Mark: Um, I guess so.

Lesley: Do you know the old saying, "*Something old, something new, something borrowed, something blue?*" I need to think about the blue part.

Mark: Isn't that just a superstition? Will there be bad luck if you don't do that?

Lesley: You never know. If it is a superstition, I believe in it.

Mark: Not me.

Lesley: What about the one about not seeing the bride before the ceremony?

Mark: That it's unlucky for the groom to see the bride in her wedding dress before the ceremony? I believe in that one. Why ask for bad luck?

Lesley: I don't think it brings bad luck. But I'll be getting ready with my sisters and girlfriends, anyway.

Mark: You know my mother told me once that it's OK for the bride to look in the mirror before she leaves for the ceremony.

Lesley: Of course. Why not?

Mark: Yeah, I agree. What I didn't know is that it was bad luck for her to look in a mirror *after* she leaves for the ceremony.

Lesley: I've never heard that.

Mark: It sounds like we're both a little superstitious about some things.

Lesley: I suppose. So where should we go on our honeymoon?

Mark: Well, if we look at the calendar and— oh, no.

Lesley: What?

Mark: Our wedding date is June 13th.

Lesley: Right. Beautiful summer weather.

Mark: That's a Friday.

Lesley: So? We don't have to get married on a weekend.

Mark: I know but, Friday the 13th?

Lesley: Oh. Oh, no. No, no, no, that's too unlucky. We *have* to change it.

Mark: I agree. I hate that day. Something bad always seems to happen.

LESSON 28

Conversation, Part C

Adam: Did you hear about those strange lights over the city on Sunday night?

Nina: No, I didn't. I was out of town.

Adam: Apparently a lot of people saw bright lights moving across the sky. They thought the lights were from a UFO.

Nina: I doubt it. It must have been a plane.

Adam: Maybe, but there were lots of them, and they were moving around in circles.

Nina: It could have been a flock of birds. Birds move around in circles sometimes.

Adam: It couldn't have been birds. Birds don't have lights attached to them! And they were really big.

Nina: Whatever it was, it couldn't have been a UFO.

Adam: Why not? How do you know?

Nina: Because there is no such thing!

LESSONS 25–28 ENGLISH IN ACTION

Eric: Tom got the advertising job at the company!!

Jill: That's amazing!

Maria: Congratulations!

Tom: Thanks guys!

Maria: I'm not sure what kind of job I want.

Eric: I'm sure you'll figure it out. Sometimes, it takes time.

Maria: You know, Jill is doing something cool these days. She's starting a blog.

Tom: That's great, Jill! What's your blog about?

Jill: It compares the different customs of the world.

Tom: That's interesting.

Jill: Yeah, did you know that in some Asian countries like Japan and Korea, you're expected to take your shoes off before entering the home?

Tom: Really?

Jill: But in America, we're expected to keep our shoes on.

Maria: That's true.

Tom: This sounds really interesting, Jill.

Jill: It's fun and I get to practice my writing. I just want to master writing.

Maria: Right. *"Jack of all trades, master of none."*

Jill: Huh?

Maria: What do you think it means?

Tom: I have no idea.

Jill: Jack of all trades is someone who can do many things…

Maria: Right. And master of none means you can't do any of the things really well. So, what would happen if Jill tried to do many different things and write?

Tom: She would be a jack of all trades, master of none.

Jill: But since my passion is writing, I should focus on that and "master" it.

Maria: Exactly!

Jill: Maria?

Maria: Yeah?

Jill: You should be a teacher.

LESSON 29
Listening, Part A

Host: Welcome to our show. I'm your host, Robin Lynn, and here in our studio is Graham Mercer. He is what you call a futurologist. Thanks for coming in.

Graham: Thanks so much for having me.

Host: Now, the term futurologist may be new to some of our listeners. What is that exactly?

Graham: Right. A futurologist is someone who discusses future events based on current events and trends. We are *not* psychic. We don't "see" the future.

Host: So, do you claim to predict the future?

Graham: Actually, no. No one can do that. What we do is suggest things that are or aren't likely.

Host: I see. But don't we all talk about and imagine the future to some extent? Isn't everyone then a futurologist?

Graham: No. We may look at and study trends and this can involve a lot of statistics. We also talk about the future based on the past and present.

Host: So, is futurology an art or science?

Graham: That's a good question. Most people actually consider it a branch of history.

Host: History? That's interesting.

Graham: It's because we look at the past and see patterns there. And consider present conditions as well. We look at how things change or stay the same. And by doing so, we map possible futures.

Host: Do you look at the future in the short-term or long-term?

Graham: Long-term. We don't look at things that will happen right away.

Host: So, you can't tell me what will be in fashion next season?

Graham: I'm afraid not.

Listening, Part B

Host: OK, I think I have a good understanding of what you do. Do you mind if I ask you some specific questions about how likely some things will be in the future?

Graham: Not at all.

Host: I read once that people will store their minds on a computer in the future. Could that really happen?

Graham: Oh, yes. I think that's quite likely. It may be 50 years away, but yes, quite likely.

Host: Wow! How about this? Will there be brain transplants?

Graham: Again, I think probably, yes, there will be. There will be a lot of changes in medicine in the future.

Host: Amazing.

Host: What about time travel? We see that in science fiction movies all the time.

Graham: I'd have to say that probably won't happen. It's a fun thing to think about, though.

Host: Let's talk more about computers. Will they have emotions?

Graham: Yes, probably. I think that one day they will be able to have feelings.

Host: Fascinating. And many people want to live forever. Is that likely?

Graham: I'd have to say no. People will live longer, that's for sure. It's happening now, but we have our limits as humans. I—

Host: Excuse me, but we need to take a quick break. We'll be right back after this word from our sponsor.

LESSON 30
Conversation, Part C

Wes: I read that they've banned plastic bottles in some European towns.

Nicki: That's a good idea. Plastic is terrible.

Wes: Why do you say that?

Nicki: Well, if they ban plastic bottles, companies will have to make glass bottles.

Wes: Are you saying glass is better than plastic?

Nicki: Yes! Glass is much better than plastic.

Wes: But why?

Nicki: Because plastic breaks down so slowly. It stays on our planet for a long time. It's bad for the environment.

Wes: But using more glass will also affect the environment. Making glass uses a lot of energy.

Nicki: I hadn't thought of that. To be honest, I don't know what the best solution is. I do think glass is prettier.

LESSON 31
Conversation, Part C

Doug: Hey, Carlos. It's Doug. Do you have any plans later?

Carlos: Um, I guess. I plan to clean my room later. Why do you ask?

Doug: Dan and Mike are having a party tonight. Mike's leaving for the summer so it's kind of a goodbye party. Lots of our friends will be there.

Carlos: It sounds fun…

Doug: Yeah. So, can you make it? Please say yes.

Carlos: Sure. I'll hurry and get all this stuff done. It won't take long.

Doug: Great. I'll pick you up. My sister is going to lend me her car.

Carlos: Really?

Doug: Yeah. I'll be going right by your dorm. What time is good?

Carlos: Anytime.

Doug: OK. I'll come around 7 p.m. I'll call when I'm there.

LESSON 32

Listening, Part A and B

1. I have never been one to set goals for myself, but I think it's a pretty good idea. I have never felt comfortable talking in front of others in a formal situation. But with my new job I knew I would have to give presentations at sales meetings, so I thought, "How can I become more confident?" So, I decided to take a public speaking class. The class is interesting so far. It's not about presentation skills, but just being comfortable talking in public. So, we practiced and practiced, and I found that's what I needed most. My friends say I'm already looking and acting more confidently.

2. I have a goal a lot of people may relate to. I mean, who doesn't want to be in better shape, right? I don't want to lose weight—I'm happy with my current weight, but I do want to get in shape. Some friends suggested joining a gym. I didn't want to do that. It can get expensive, and it's hard to find the time sometimes. So I just started jogging with my friends. It's easy, fun, and it helps a lot to run with another person. That can be very motivating. I'm already starting to feel the results.

3. I have an OK job, but I feel like I don't manage my money very well. I wish I could do that better. I never seem to know how much money I have, or where it ends up going. I try to watch it but I'm busy, and to be honest I don't really know how to manage my money. There is a class on money management near my office that meets twice a week. I thought about taking that but it's kind of expensive. I found an online class I'm planning to take. It has budget tools, an online coach, and a chat room where others taking the class can talk about what works for them. I've never taken an online class before—hope I like it!

4. Have you ever seen those ads on TV about how you can be financially independent in three easy steps? Well, that is a goal of mine—to be financially independent, but I don't trust those ads. I wasn't sure what the best way to achieve that was, so I asked around and did some research. It's all about getting the right information and making informed decisions. I got a coach to help me. You set a very specific goal, which I did, and this person helps you achieve it step by step. My coach isn't cheap, but I think it's the best way to see results.

LESSONS 29–32 ENGLISH IN ACTION

Jill: I can't believe you're moving out!

Maria: It seems like we met just yesterday!

Eric: I know. But hey, we will definitely see each other.

Maria: Hopefully, I get a job around here, too.

Tom: Of course you will!

Jill: Eric, why are you throwing that glass bottle away?

Eric: What? I don't need it. I prefer plastic bottles anyway.

Maria: Plastic breaks down extremely slowly.

Jill: Yeah. Keep it. You can use it later.

Eric: OK. That's a really good idea.

Tom: Do you guys think laptops will exist in twenty years?

Maria: No, people won't use laptops because there will be large computer screens that look like TVs everywhere! People will be able to use the computers anytime they want, so they won't need their own!

Eric: Wow. That sounds cool. Have you guys thought about what life will be like in the future? Maybe, cars will finally fly!

Jill: I think cars will run from energy in plants.

Tom: Twenty years from now, I think things will be just as they are now.

Maria: Maybe, but things can't be exactly the same. Things are changing so quickly these days.

Tom: That is true…hey, Eric. What should I do with the stuff inside your desk?

Eric: I plan to clean my desk later.

Tom: OK.

Maria: What are all your goals in twenty years?

Tom: I want to have a family and have a really cool job where I travel around a lot.

Eric: I hope I've found the cure for cancer.

Maria: I want to have my own place and be financially independent.

Jill: I want to have my own website with millions of visitors.

Eric: What if they don't have websites in twenty years?

Maria: It might be something else!

Jill: Maybe, one of us will think of something better!

Maria: You guys want to get coffee?

Eric/ Jill: Sounds good! OK!

Tom: Yes, before coffee becomes a thing of the past!

Vocabulary Index

LESSON 13
bully
checkers
childhood
hopscotch *классики*
playground
tomboy *сорванец*
zoo

LESSON 14
awful
disgusting
embarrassing
lucky
romantic
scary
strange

LESSON 15
cancel
catch
cause
close
crash
deny
donate
save
score *зол*

LESSON 16
celebrity scandal
daring rescue
key discovery
natural disaster
political change
royal wedding
sporting success

LESSON 17
acquaintance
best friend
childhood friend
fair-weather friend
former friend
lifelong friend
old friend

LESSON 18
accepting
caring
forgiving
loyal
reliable
supportive
truthful

LESSON 19
do volunteer work
go to social events
introduce yourself
join an online group
join a student club
make friends through friends
play sports
take a class
use social networks

LESSON 20
apologize
feelings
ignore
involved
joke
problem

LESSON 21
communication skills
computer skills
fluency in English
good school grades
graduate degree
knowledge of current affairs
leadership
overseas experience
work experience

LESSON 22
amusement park
bus line
fast food
hair coloring
office supplies
online travel service
soft drink

LESSON 23
airlines
banks
convenience stores
department stores
language schools
shopping malls
supermarkets

LESSON 24
idea
location
logo
marketing
price
service

OXFORD
UNIVERSITY PRESS

198 Madison Avenue
New York, NY 10016 USA

Great Clarendon Street, Oxford, OX2 6DP, United Kingdom

Oxford University Press is a department of the University of Oxford.
It furthers the University's objective of excellence in research, scholarship,
and education by publishing worldwide. Oxford is a registered trade
mark of Oxford University Press in the UK and in certain other countries.

General Manager, American ELT: Laura Pearson
Executive Publishing Manager: Erik Gundersen
Managing Editor: Jennifer Meldrum
Associate Editor: Hana Yoo
Director, ADP: Susan Sanguily
Executive Design Manager: Maj-Britt Hagsted
Associate Design Manager: Michael Steinhofer
Image Manager: Trisha Masterson
Art Editor: Joe Kassner
Electronic Production Manager: Julie Armstrong
Production Artist: Elissa Santos
Production Coordinator: Brad Tucker

ISBN: 978 0 19 403017 5 Speak Now Student Book 3 (PACK)
ISBN: 978 0 19 403002 1 Speak Now Student Book 3 (PACK COMPONENT)
ISBN: 978 0 19 403023 6 SPEAK NOW Access Card 3 (PACK COMPONENT)
ISBN: 978 0 19 403026 7 SPEAK NOW Online Practice 3 (PACK COMPONENT)

Printed in China
This book is printed on paper from certified and well-managed sources

ACKNOWLEDGEMENTS

Illustrations by: Barb Bastian: 15, 54; Kenneth Batelman: 17; Bunky Hurter: 18,
34, 56, 74; Neil Jeffrey: 14, 32; Javier Joaquin: 4, 25, 64; Gavin Reece: 24, 48.

Commissioned photography by: Richard Hutchings/Digital Light Source, Cover
photo of person speaking and cast shot on page ii; People's Television, Inc., all
video stills.

*The publishers would like to thank the following for their kind permission to reproduce
photographs:* Cover (Grand Canyon) Momatiuk - Eastcott/Corbis, (diver)
Stephen Frink/CORBIS, (Ballet) Roger Bamber /Alamy, (background montage)
PhotoAlto/Sigrid Olsson/Getty images, Howard Kingsnorth/Cultura/Getty
images, Christopher Futcher/istockphoto.com, Fabrice LEROUGE/Getty
images, PhotoAlto/Getty images, Andresr/shutterstock.com, Monkey Business
Images/shutterstock.com, Ferran Traite Soler/istockphoto.com, PhotoAlto/
Sigrid Olsson/Getty images; pg. 2 Bader-Butowski/Westend61/Corbis; pg. 3
Ariel Skelley/Blend Images/Getty Images; pg. 5 Paul Harizan/StockImage/Getty
Images; pg. 6 (Sara) StockLite/shutterstock.com, (Keisha) Jack Hollingsworth/
Blend Images/Getty Images, (Keisha and Kelly) Jack Hollingsworth/Blend
Images/Getty Images; pg. 7 Digital Vision/Oxford University Press; pg. 8
(Megan) BestPhotoStudio/shutterstock.com, (Derek) Mark Farwell/Stockbyte/
Getty Images; pg. 9 AIMSTOCK/istockphoto.com; pg. 12 Fuse/Getty Images;
pg. 13 Nikada/istockphoto.com; pg. 16 (Clerk) Reza Estakhrian/Stone/Getty
Images, (Guest) Harry Vorsteher/Corbis; pg. 19 Ilona Baha/shutterstock.com;
pg. 22 Andrey Bayda/shutterstock.com; pg. 23 Tobias Helbig/istockphoto.
com; pg. 25 UpperCut Images/Getty Images; pg. 26 (receptionist) Stewart
Cohen/Pam Ostrow/Blend Images/Corbis, (Heather) DreamPictures/Shannon
Faulk/Blend Images/Getty Images; pg. 27 dp Photography/shutterstock.com;
pg. 28 (Calvin) East/shutterstock.com, (Ben) Edyta Pawlowska/shutterstock.
com, (Venice) Vladimir Sklyarov/shutterstock.com; pg. 29 Robert Clare/Taxi/
Getty Images; pg. 33 debr22pics/shutterstock.com; pg. 35 Garry Gay / Alamy;
pg. 35 Danil Melekhin/istockphoto.com;pg. 38 (Glen) BestPhotoStudio/
shutterstock.com, (Allie) Alejandro Rivera/istockphoto.com, (Harry Potter
poster) WARNER BROS. PICTURES / Album/Newscom; pg. 39 Jonathan Larsen/
Diadem Images / Alamy; pg. 42 (Kal) Gareth Boden/Oxford University Press,
(Winnie) Glow Images/Getty Images; pg. 43 Rolf Bruderer/Blend Images/Getty
Images; pg. 44 © Eric Audras/PhotoAlto/Corbis; pg. 45 Fancy / Alamy; pg. 46
Suprijono Suharjoto/istockphoto.com; pg. 47 holbox/shutterstock.com; pg.
49 Westend61 GmbH / Alamy; pg. 52 Alexander Raths/shutterstock.com; pg.
53 Kristian Gehradte/istockphoto.com; pg. 54 (Travelocity ad) Eric Goodwin
KRT/Newscom, (John) Mathias Wilson/istockphoto.com, (Amanda) qingqing/
shutterstock.com, (woman in hair ad) YuriyZhuravov/shutterstock.com; pg.
55 Brandon Bourdages/shutterstock.com; pg. 57 Cheng Xin/istockphoto.com;
pg. 58 (Carmen) Golden Pixels LLC/shutterstock.com, (Greg) Neustockimages/
istockphoto.com; pg. 59 Jarno Gonzalez Zarraonandia/shutterstock.com;
pg. 62 auremar/shutterstock.com; pg. 63 Nikola Spasenoski/istockphoto.
com; pg. 65 Dawn Hudson/istockphoto.com; pg. 66 Sagel & Kranefeld/Corbis;
pg. 67 Peter Titmuss / Alamy; pg. 68 (Adam) Factoria Singular/istockphoto.
com, (Nina) Yuri Arcurs/shutterstock.com; pg. 69 Colin McPherson/Sygma/
Corbis; pg. 72 (Katie) lev dolgachov/shutterstock.com, (Engineer) Iryna Rasko/
shutterstock.com, (car) Maksonix/shutterstock.com; pg. 73 Darren Baker/
shutterstock.com; pg. 74 Robert Becker/istockphoto.com; pg. 75 Denis Tabler/
shutterstock.com; pg. 76 (Doug) Jonny le Fortune/F1online/Getty Images,
(Carlos) ansar80/istockphoto.com; pg. 77 S.Borisov/shutterstock.com; pg. 78
Pedro Salaverría/shutterstock.com; pg. 79 (a) Chase Jarvis/Digital Vision/Getty
Images, (b) Paul Bradbury/OJO Images/Getty Images, (c) moodboard / Alamy,
(d) AVAVA/shutterstock.com, (goals) marekuliasz/shutterstock.com; pg. 85
Fuse/Getty Images; pg. 86 MM Productions/Lifesize/Getty Images.

Additional photography provided by: Asia Images Group Pte Ltd/Alamy, Aldo
Murillo/istockphoto.com, Neustockimages/istockphoto.com (speaking images
in top border); DPiX Center/shutterstock.com (brushed metal texture in
side border).

Video: People's Television, Inc. / www.ppls.tv